The Tailgater's Handbook

Joe Drozda

mp
MASTERS PRESS

A Division of Howard W. Sams & Company
A Bell Atlantic Company

Published by Masters Press
A Division of Howard W. Sams & Company,
A Bell Atlantic Company
2647 Waterfront Pkwy E. Dr, Suite 300
Indianapolis, IN 46214

96 97 98 99 00 01   10 9 8 7 6 5 4 3 2 1

Library of Congress Cataloging-in-Publication Data

Drozda, Joe—
    The tailgater's handbook / Joe Drozda.
        p. cm.
    ISBN: 1-57028-093-2 (trade paper)
    1. Tailgate parties -- United States. 2. Tailgate parties--United States
    -- History. 3. Football fans -- United States -- Social life and customs. I. Title.

GV1472. D76 1996   96-20384
                                    CIP

Dedication

This book is dedicated to all the people who live for Saturdays in the fall, those individuals who plan their business and personal engagements around the football schedule, experience a rise in their body temperature when they enter the stadium, feel a tear during the alma mater and know the words to the fight song. It is for people who wake up very early on the Sunday after a win, just to read each and every one of the stories about the game they saw. It is for all those who enjoy good company and good food in the parking lot as much, if not more, than the food and company at a fancy restarant.

What's Inside

Acknowledgements

I would like to thank:

My wife Cindy, for all the questions and read-throughs.

My daughter Tricia for the better art in this book, and both she and her brother Joe for surveying tailgaters on occasion.

My mother Bozena, for her help with the initial research.

My Aunt Jean Milonski, for her help with some recipes.

The research staff at the Brownsburg, Indiana library for their never-ending assistance: Kristina Daily-Brothers, an Illini alumna, who was my sounding board; smiling Sarah Wright, an Indiana grad, who knows every call number without a computer; DePauw's Rachel Bowen, who can track most anything down and Nancy Gwin, Manchester College, who really knows Info Trac but doesn't approve of alumni wasting money on sports. I'll bet none of them believed this book would ever get done.

Joe and Sue Carey, our tailgating partners. Joe has consumed 35,000 olives and four ounces of vermouth in his long life.

My editor, Holly Kondras, who had the patience of Job in dealing with me, and the "sports freaks" at Masters. Her boss, Tom Bast, for liking my handbook concept.

Kim Blanchar, etymologist, and Charlie Brockman, scout.

The nice people from the great companies that trusted me to finish this book. People like Lee Stranahthan of Igloo, Mark Wildman and Dick Leinenkugel from Miller Brewing and Leinies, Norb Lyons of Syroco, Ronald Sack and Rinaldo Manago of Charbroil. Also Charles McIlwaine and Carolyn Britton of Coleman, Alexis Limberakis and Carol Plisch of Kingsford and Matchlight, John Pepper of Rubbermaid, Greg Lawrie of Candea, and Dennis McCormick of Academy Broadway.

The many hundreds of people who posed for pictures, answered questionnaires, and sent recipes. Your sharing of ideas, opinions and secrets is going to help a lot of tailgaters.

Cathy Robinson, for her personal efforts to help. Her smile comes through the phone lines.

Ike Maggert, "There's No Other Place Like Nebraska." See you down the road.

The friends, staffs and SIDs from over a hundred of the great Colleges and Universities of America. There are just too many to fit here. Extra thanks to Steve Snapp of Ohio State, Kenny

Klein and Kathy Tronso of Louisville, Greg Elkin and Kit Klingelhofer at Indiana, David Leppla, Sharon Martin and Jim Vruggink of Purdue, Tom Porter at Illinois, John Heisler of Notre Dame, Langton Rogers of Ole Miss, Kevin McKinney of Wyoming, Mike Whitaker of the Clemson Sports Network, Bud Ford of Tennesse and Dave Kellogg of Air Force.

David Finch, T.S.T.G.W.A.J.B.T., a real Northwestern grad at Johnsonville. Peter Klamka of Wilshire Fragrance, the John and Carey Aron of the Pasta Shoppe in Nashville, and Mark Tarner of The South Bend Chocolate Company.

Richard Brookhiser and Marie Simmons for allowing me to quote their writings. *The Sporting News*, *Financial World Magazine*, *The Purdue Alumnus*, Chapters Publishers, *The Inside Edge Magazine* and the Indiana Bureau of Motor Vehicles for their contributions.

And finally, thanks to Dick and Linda Truxel in the mountains and Jim and Shirley Wilmot in the "North Woods" for the spare beds, good food and better fellowship.

The Tailgater's Handbook

For Starters

College football is and always has been, the nation's greatest spectator sport. Pro football, by contrast, has almost become a creation of television. It seems to exist to sell commercials, licensed products and whatever else the TV networks want to promote. Tradition is to college football what money is to professional football.

The interdependence of pro football and television is so complete that it seems the American public cannot have one without the other. The same TV that gave us two-year murder trials, in-your-face shoe and jean commercials now shows computer-enhanced and animated graphics that look like clips from those futuristic gladiator movies just to introduce a pro football game. Television sports personalities promote the next sitcom during games, and hosts try to hype football on non-sport programs. Is there anything more annoying than to have a network morning show host, on remote location at the site of the game, perform some stupid stunt to show everyone who watches that the Super Bowl is next Sunday on this network? Do you get tired of a group of people on a TV screen spending an hour, between too many commercials, preparing you to watch a preseason football game? A game where the question remains, "Do the players even care who wins?"

College football, by contrast, is trips to a scenic campus in the fall, surrounded by the beautiful foliage.

College football is cheerleaders,
trips to a scenic campus,
and excited fans in school colors

It's the sounds made by bands marching to the stadium through endless rows of excited fans dressed in school colors. It's cheerleaders, students, the fight song, button-down shirts, and playing the rival school's team. It's what forces famous men like Yale's Coach Tad Jones to utter, "Gentlemen, you are now going to play football against Harvard. Never again in your whole life will you do anything so important."

Pro football is TV cameras viewing the "Haves" in luxury suites, drinking champagne, looking down on the "Have Not's", sitting in the regular seats, drinking beer, watching the players on the field who unsnap their helmets and walk back to their huddle. This modern generation of players taught us how to taunt and celebrate in a fashion which can almost be tied to TV marketing. They've taught our sons to wear earrings and use bad grammar.

In college the players have real emotion for the game. They run onto the field, jump up and down, inspire their student sections and "give it the good old college try." They gave us the end zone prayer; they wear ties on game day and play in front of alumni who attend games almost as often during losing seasons as they do when the team is winning.

Some people say that college football is the minor league system for the pros. If that's true, have them tell you if there is any other "minor league" that outdraws the majors. In the 1994-95 season, for example, the top 28 college teams outdrew the 28 pro teams by an average of more than 14,000 people per game. What pro team can boast the support of Penn State, Michigan, Ohio State, Tennessee, or Florida? On September 23, 1995, more than 166,000 people attended college football games in the state of Indiana. This is just one day, in one state, with no extremely large crowds. Every Saturday in the fall, there are many other states that draw more.

Some fans say that the pros are more exciting because they have the great passers, receivers and defenses. But colleges have all that and the double reverse, the wishbone, the onside kick, the 99 yard run and the tie.

College also has the "Old Charlie", the alum whose eyes have tears during the alma mater, whose season ticket number is 43,555, whose tailgate menu is set by Tuesday, whose son is a star at "home town high" and who comes to the game because of love. It is the love of his school and his memories of the time he spent there that bring them. They love to recall singing these songs, walking these grounds and the time when they had everything in the world to look forward to. That is college football. That is Saturday in the fall in America. That is what this book is about.

*College football is tailgating, good food,
good friends and the fight song being
played by a real band*

Tailgating Takes off

How did tailgating get its start? Richard Brookhiser (Yale '77) wrote a humorous article entitled "How The Gate Got its Tail" for *Forbes*. Brookhiser gives us the following historical setting:

In 1904 there were six special trains with some 54 private cars arriving for the Harvard-Yale game. In this party were the Vice President Elect, Charles W. Fairbanks rooting for Yale, and Alice Lee Roosevelt, daughter of the President, rooting for Harvard. The New York Times reported how "refinement, culture and an easy disposition were written" on the faces of the crowd.

As these fans arrived at the stadium they got hungry, what could they do? Have the staff lay something out, obviously. But where? Their trains were all the way back at the station. "Hence over time the tailgate, which makes use of a more accessible surface, evolved."

I imagine that the evolution might have progressed along the lines that follow:

The fans at the 1904 Harvard -Yale game included a Mr. and Mrs. Robert B. Winthrup III, who, after leaving the train, got hungry. Robert decided to purchase something from a vender. His choices were hardly the Dove bars or Uno's Pizza of today. His options were hot dogs, peanuts, coffee and lemonade; not very appetizing to someone used to daily lunches at his private club consisting of choices like Welsh Rarebit, squab, or roast beef! Something would have to be done if Robert and his bride Katherine were to survive future games.

Katherine suggested that the "help" could make up a basket for the next excursion to include those beautiful fried chickens they took to the shore last summer. And, perhaps a blanket for sitting upon to eat could double as a stadium blanket. Her mouth watered as she imagined the chicken, rolls, potato salad, fresh fruit and pie. Great idea, but she forgot something.

After the feast, what could they do with the basket during the game? Since the early Ivy teams were the national powers, the small stadiums were always full (Harvard's new stadium was a year away and Yale's bowl a decade from completion). Robert was going to have to hold that picnic basket the whole game. Poor Katherine was understandably at her wit's end. Robert eventually paid an undergraduate to watch the basket for them. After the game he got it back, empty.

Robert suggested that, for the next game, they have their car

brought to the station to deliver Katherine's party (she invited friends) and their picnic baskets to the stadium. The car would provide shelter as well as livery service. What a great idea, except to William, their driver, who usually had that weekend off and now got to race the train all the way up to New Haven!

Locals who didn't arrive by train, noticing Robert and Katherine and other picnickers, exclaimed, "What a great idea!" More and more people planned to join the fun by driving to the next game and bringing their own picnics.

As in everything successful Americans do, there is an instinct which urges them to improve activities they repeat. Thus, the picnic basket and blanket were augmented by the car hood. Eventually folding tables and chairs were added. Around 1930 a fan arrived at a game with a new station wagon. The invention of the station wagon finally provided a real tailgate. This tailgate allowed the access to food in the rear of the vehicle and made a perfect table. People like Bob IV (Robert III's son) had to have one as well. The roomy wagon allowed Bob and Lynn, his bride, to really expand their picnics.

Eventually these younger Winthrups' began to experiment with more and more elaborate pregame meals. They also got a chance to experience an outdoor dining joy known as food poisoning. Bob's lust

for liver paté and Lynn's Waldorf salad were well aged by game time. Consequently the Winthrups and most of their tailgate guests found their fun dampened by many trips to scarce rest rooms.

The choice for our tailgaters became either to avoid many desired dishes or find a solution to safely store food before serving. Even cave men knew that foods kept cold would not spoil. Initially, to keep things cold, a block of ice was used. Ice was heavy and messy, but it would keep most foods from spoiling and it would go well in drinks when chipped with an ice pick. Carrying a heavy dripping block of ice in a tub proved, however, to be difficult for William who was still driving for the family in his 70s.

The Winthrups then turned to the camping industry. Bob, who considered himself a man of the people, had an employee down at his factory who was an avid camper. This worker, Patsy Savatini, an Italian fellow with a huge family, was one of Bob's favorites. Patsy found through his camping activities a "portable" ice chest and also a little portable stove. He shared the products with Bob who liked them so well that he bought the company! And, more important the Winthrups discovered that it was possible to prepare, or at least serve, great varieties of foods safely in the stadium parking lot!

After "the war" the United States experienced a transportation boom.

Automobiles became affordable to the average citizen and airlines began to take away railroad passengers. It took a while, but eventually rail passenger service disappeared (except for commuter trains). People had to provide their own transportation to campus. The family car was up to the task and also allowed the carrying of tailgating supplies and equipment for the less wealthy fans and alumni. That's when Rob V (Bob's son) and the newest Mrs. Winthrup, Alice, watched a young star named Pat Savatini play fullback and score the game winning touchdown.

Rob and Alice were very warm and cordial people. They met the Savatini family in the stadium parking lot. They were an interesting group who's father, it turns out worked for Rob's dad when he owned the factory. What a small world!

Rob and Alice weren't much for tradition. When William died, they didn't even hire a new driver. They actually drove themselves. And when the Savatinis introduced them to sausage sandwiches cooked in the parking lot with lots of onions and peppers, the tailgate menu was adjusted forever. Mustard replaced the caviar and bottles of beer replaced champagne. After all, times were changing.

The Ivies were talking about de-emphasizing sports. Schools from places way out West began to take over "big time" football. These were institutions like Pittsburgh, Ohio State, Purdue and even California.

Today, the latest Winthrups, Robbie VI and Ashley, still tailgate, but at a catholic school all the way out in South Bend, Indiana. Most of the colleges they visit seem to encourage tailgating. They provide special areas and incentives for picnickers. There are contests and even school supplied party tents. Most stadiums even have toilets in the parking lots for the comfort of the fans. Robbie, while enjoying a beer, wondered if any of the previous generations of Winthrups ever thought about doing something neat like tailgating.

The Seven P's

(Types of Tailgaters)

The Partier

Some tailgaters are very, very serious partiers. They want to be at a party whenever possible. "This is Saturday so the party is at the game." They see a limitless potential for a party in the parking lot. They tend to enlist as many friends as possible for their tailgate. They always have a good time and sometimes don't even go into the stadium. This type of tailgater can be an undergraduate. In the case of students, however, the menu planner will substitute beer and McDonalds or KFC for cocktails and gourmet food. Although the Partier can be a gourmand or a lush or both, he doesn't have to be. Partiers are interested in the tailgate as a "social event."

The Pretender

Other tailgaters are hooked into it. They are only here because someone, who did their thinking for them, decided that "everyone" was going to the game. If left to their own devices

they wouldn't be at the game at all or they would arrive late and leave early. Their idea of a great football event is the annual Super Bowl party in the family room of their boss. Their biggest problem is to figure what to wear. Pretenders sometimes ask fans in front of them at games to sit down, even after touchdowns by the home team. (They are the ones who bring an umbrella into the stadium.)

The Politician

The politician is easy to spot in the parking lot. He's the one who always has a smile on his face and seems to be looking into the distance for some-one to say hello to (even when shaking your hand). Politicians will not tailgate on a day when the weather is bad or when there is an event to attend where they will be more visible.

The Pusher

We all have some traits in common with the pusher, but some are worse than others. If the pusher is a heavy drinker, he enjoys offering drinks. In fact he is downright depressed if someone isn't drinking. If he's a big eater he wants everyone to eat, plenty! "Hey, it's game day, you can splurge a little." He once bought the house a round at a doughnut shop.

The Perpetual Sophomore

He is always dressed to the nines in the school colors and his sweatshirt has the latest in super graphics. He plays fight songs, flies flags, throws toilet paper at the games, leads cheers and, in general, has as much fun as an undergraduate.

The Practical Engineer

These tailgaters are always designing something to make their tailgate bet-

ter. They have neat things that are not readily available like flagpole holders, carriers, odd flags, homemade tents, port-o-lets, and grills. Everything fits like pieces of a puzzle into their vehicle.

The Peaked Tailgater

Is a person who is little less of a perpetual tailgater than he or she used to be. He now misses a few games. He still knows how to do it right, but other things sometimes prevent him from attending the Saturday picnic or staying after the game. He has a bottle of Ibuprofen in his tailgate bar.

Why Do People Tailgate?

Surveyed over a two year period were hundreds of people tailgating in parking lots at college games. The first question asked was what is the most fun thing about tailgating? Here are the answers:

Socializing with friends,
family, etc..71%
Eating neat, delicious food..................13%
Drinking...7%
Watching the opposite sex....................4%
Being Outdoors.....................................2%
Partying...1%
Cooking...1%
Flag raising..1%
           TOTAL.................100%

Our surveyors

Tailgaters Are Born, Not Made

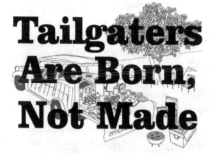

Children born to a couple who are serious tailgaters have the good fortune to grow up attending college football games. At least they do as soon as they are old enough to tolerate the several hours of a game and travel. The first song they know all the words to is the school fight song. They grow up with every possible piece of merchandise made in the appropriate colors with the school logo. They acquire sweatshirts, hats, scarves, music boxes that play the alma mater, frisbees, rain gear and things like rubber training pants that proclaim school loyalty like "I'm behind the Tigers."

Children of tailgaters grow up with the memory of being spoiled by Mom and Dad on Saturdays. The family menu is planned after consulting everyone, including the kids. Families that hardly ever eat meat during the week blow it on Saturday's tailgate by cooking juicy, delicious brats. Fearing child boredom on the trip, the folks generally have drinks, snacks and candy in the vehicle. The parents even

pack things like frisbees, hand-held video games, and footballs for entertainment before the game while food is being prepared.

These kids learn and become comfortable with the ins and outs of football and tailgating. They grow up referring to their mom's and dad's school as "us" or "we." They look forward to tailgating on Saturdays. That is until the time when peers and school activities prevent them from accompanying the parents on Saturdays.

There are conflicts like prep football, SAT tests, sleeping or new friends who think tailgating is uncool. These conflicts cause them to miss an occasional Saturday trip to campus. They miss a few more games and then a whole season until finally they decide they don't want to tailgate anymore, ever! Their "tailgating urge" has become dormant. It may not resurface for years.

As undergraduates, they attend the college of their parents, but they aren't really tailgaters again. Their parent's tailgate is just like home,

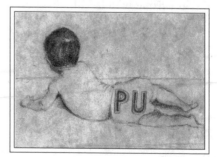

A born Purdue fan

always there, with plenty of food and money, but not exciting enough for them to invest the whole day. The real party is with the members of the opposite sex in the student section and after the game.

Eventually these children of tailgaters become alumni and on some fall Saturday they'll make the beautiful drive to campus for the "big game." They'll see tailgaters and somewhere, repressed in their memory, the thought will surface that they belong in this picture. Sort of like "déjà vu, all over again." They'll make plans to tailgate at the next football game. Usually returning to tailgating with another couple or friends on a small scale, they eventually escalate their preparations. And when they start a family of their own, the cycle begins anew.

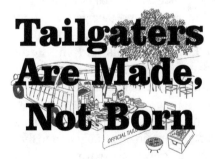

Tailgaters Are Made, Not Born

Tailgaters are made not born. They grow up with parents who may have never attended college or college football games. These people are first exposed to tailgating as undergraduates. They observe tailgaters while walking through the parking lot on their way to the student section inside the stadium. They pass people who seem to have it made.

These rich (everyone looks rich to an undergraduate) alumni park their big, freshly waxed Lincolns, Mercedes and motor homes near the stadium. These vehicles reflect the blue of the early fall sky. Compared to normal student cars (old Chevys and Fords), this parking area looks like a luxury car lot or the outside of a Country Club. However, the contents of these cars and vans are even more impressive to the average undergraduate.

Alumni are standing about wearing expensive-looking sweaters and plaid slacks in school colors. They drink cocktails and spread gourmet foods on Pendleton wool blankets. They look tan and happy as they hand their kids cash and beer.

The students talk about their fellow classmates as they go by, saying things like, "There's John Smith III, he's president of Phi Gamma Delta and he's on the tennis team. His old man played in the Rose Bowl back in '62, and he's President of the biggest bank in Chicago. That's his van painted in school colors."

Somewhere in this scene the thought is conceived by one of these future bank presidents, "When I become an alum I am going to be spending my Saturdays just like them."

Clothes Make the Man

(and the Tailgater)

College tailgaters dress very well. They have to, because they never know who's going to walk by their party; perhaps an old fraternity brother/sorority sister or classmate may make an appearance. They don't want to appear unsuccessful. The other reason college tailgaters dress well is that they are almost all college grads who have been taught to "dress for success." They buy more expensive clothes. (See the Commandments of Tailgating.)

The Top Ten Best Smelling Fans*

1. Indiana
2. Penn State
3. Kentucky
4. Michigan
5. Florida
6. Alabama
7. Texas
8. Connecticut
9. Florida State
10. Texas A&M

*These rankings are derived from sales figures from the Campus Collection by Wilshire Fragrances, Inc. These fans bought the most bottles of licensed cologne.

The first stop in shopping for a tailgate wardrobe should be your college's book store or gift center (either in person or by catalog). Here is where you can get all the official logo clothes in top quality. They have the fitted wool baseball caps and official logo sweaters in cashmere, cotton or wool. Their golf/polo shirts are real cotton. They also have clothing items that other stores can't afford to stock. An example would be an orange and blue regimental striped silk tie. Not a big call for this item at the Men's Wearhouse, I guarantee it! But the Illini Bookstore in Champaign probably sells some every week.

Nice generic clothing, because of price, should not be bought from the college bookstore any more than one should shop for Christmas at the airport concourse giftorama. Other stores like Jos. A. Bank have the plaid wool slacks, the khakis, blue button downs, ties and sweaters in better selections with at least as good a price. L.L. Bean, Land's End and Eddie Bauer have these same clothes even cheaper in their catalogs and their exchange and refund policies are fantastic. It is acceptable to bring one of these catalogs to a tailgate and they make good additions for the bathroom library as well.

Items like rain ponchos (no tailgater ever takes an umbrella into a stadium), pins/buttons that play music, and other novelty or accessory items can be bought wherever the price is best.

Pictured here are some of the Campus Collection by Wilshire Fragrances, Inc. of Merrimack, NH. These are not all the same cologne in different bottles, so a family with a Michigan State and a Michigan alumnus would not have to worry that they smelled alike. There are officially licensed colognes for most major colleges. Fans can call Wilshire direct at (800) 764-1042 or find their school's cologne at their favorite local department store.

Discount stores usually have a nice display for the local colleges as football season begins.

In the early fall, tailgaters will wear mainly cotton: shirts with slacks or skirts and sweaters or sweatshirts for late in the day. As the football season progresses, the need for warmer attire becomes evident. The smart fans layer their clothing and incorporate more wool and nylon into the wardrobe. However, no matter what the weather, the important thing is to dress colorfully with a sense of tradition and class.

A windproof jacket of a simple solid color, of course, over a sweater or sweatshirt over a shirt and undershirt will provide enough warmth for games from Wisconsin (Minnesota has a 70 degree dome) to Maine. The nylon breaks the wind and the layers allow flexibility. For slacks, a fan can wear sweat pants under or over a pair of cords. If it is so cold that all thought of fashion is gone, like a bowl game in Memphis on December 31st when it is 20 degrees, go ahead and wear the sweats on the outside. If it's warmer, in daylight, wear them underneath. Veteran tailgaters seem to have a sixth sense which tells them when it's OK to look warm instead of looking stylish.

Tailgaters Are Expert Travelers

How far did you drive to get to "today's game"? What's the furthest you've traveled to tailgate? These burning questions headed a survey of hundreds of tailgaters at several major universities.

The average tailgater traveled 91.9 miles to the game they were attending when surveyed. The longest drive was by Steve Linn, a Purdue grad. He drove 506 miles from Indianapolis to Pennsylvania. Steve, in true Purdue fashion, wrote his survey answers using a beer can for a writing surface. His labored writing script was probably caused by a combination of the can, the contents of the can, and his long drive.

We found that fans on the average drove more miles to games if their campus was in a college town rather than in a large city. The reason is simple. There are more fans and alumni close to campus in big cities. For example, Louisville and Ohio State fans surveyed generally travel very short distances to the game. While fans at schools like Indiana, Notre Dame, Penn State and even Illinois tended to drive a hundred miles or more.

Most long term tailgaters take or have taken a road trip or two to a far away game. The longest distance traveled to tailgate averaged at 376 miles. Ohio State fan Bob Bulen went the farthest tailgating at the Rose Bowl 2000 miles from his home in suburban Columbus, Ohio. Also, Iowa fans Bill Weiland and Bruce White traveled to Pasadena (not together) to tailgate outside the Rose Bowl; that's approximately 1600 miles from home.

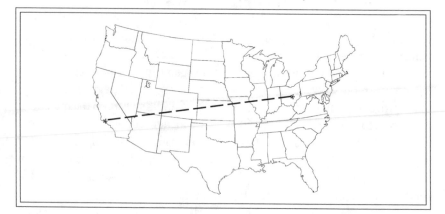

Top 30 Tailgating Schools

The following list contains the top tailgating schools in America. These ratings are based on scores from our survey of athletic departments as well as personal visits and information obtained from interviews. Factors considered were encouragement of tailgating, availability of parking, toilet facilities, donor privileges, special group tailgating, attendance at games, tolerance of alcohol, size of tailgating areas, parking surfaces, esthetics and the practice of road-trip tailgating.

1. Georgia	11. Indiana	21. Mississippi
2. Louisville	12. Purdue	22. Wyoming
3. Ohio State	13. South Carolina	23. Army
4. Illinois	14. Florida	24. E. Carolina
5. Penn State	15. Auburn	25. N. Carolina State
6. Michigan	16. Colorado	26. Air Force
7. Notre Dame	17. Maryland	27. Texas Tech
8. Nebraska	18. Oregon	28. Washington
9. LSU	19. Northwestern	29. Rice
10. Clemson	20. Iowa State	30. Wake Forest

Honorable Mentions:

Georgia Tech
Iowa
Wisconsin
Michigan State
Tennessee
Northern Illinois
Oklahoma State

"How 'bout them Dawgs?"
— ah, those Georgia tailgaters!

The Road Trip

OFFICIAL TAILGATER

Tailgaters generally don't go to road games. They become comfortable with regular surroundings in their own parking area with their usual friends, lot attendants and security personnel. They get familiar with leaving home at the same hour every home game Saturday. They know when to stow their picnic away so that they can get into the stadium in time for the pregame band renditions of the fight song, alma mater, and the entrance of the team. It's hard to know what to expect when you're on the road.

Most road trips, except those to the cross state rival, are arranged because of friendships with people from the opposing school. Usually there is an overnight stay with these friends and then a joint tailgate on Saturday. Thus, tailgaters on the road don't have their own kitchen along with many of the other regular items and amenities. Their contribution to the party will probably be the drinks or a store bought fruit or cheese basket. What is special, however, is the comradeship of people from opposing schools tailgating together. The contrasting colors of clothes and the

Top Five College Towns

Here are The Sporting News' *1995 Top Five College Football Towns and some of the reasons for their standing.*

1. **South Bend, IN**. New home of the College Football Hall of Fame. Old home of the House That Knute Built (and Lou Remodeled). Actually has a bar in sight of the stadium called the Linebacker Lounge. Hear the sizzle of burgers on the outdoor grills on Saturday mornings. Feel the sizzle course through the campus.

2. **Auburn, AL.** When the crowd in the stadium is a couple times the size of the town, you're in the right place. Jordan-Hare Stadium rocks! Toomer's Corner rolls! Witness Tiger Walk from the dorm to the stadium, and take ear plugs.

3. **Lincoln, NE.** More than three decades of sellouts before the best fans in the game.

4. **Tallahasse, FL.** More car flags per capita than any crowd in the nation. As hospitable as Bobby Bowden, unless you're wearing orange and blue.

5. **Ann Arbor, MI.** Maize-and-blue everything. Stand in line at the Cottage Inn, which has the best pizza in the Big Ten, if not in Division 1-A. Michigan Stadium is built like the Rose Bowl, only bigger, which is why the Wolverines feel at home in Pasadena.

byplay before the game are fun and memorable.

If a tailgater decides to take a trip to a road game with his own equipment and attempts to tailgate just like at home, he needs to plan ahead. There are questions that need answers before taking the trip. Does the home university tolerate drinking? Is there parking space to tailgate? What time do they need to arrive for a good location? What menu will lend itself to travel, preparation, storage or purchase at the destination? For answers to these and other concerns, try seeking assistance from the opposing school's ticket office, the town's Chamber of Commerce, or, better yet, the local friend you discover while looking through your school alumni directory.

The rule of thumb is to keep it simple. Take necessary items only. Take the flags and pole so that you make a statement and other fans from your school will see you and stop by. Take the compact folding picnic table instead of the large table with separate chairs. Take a portable gas grill and your folding Coleman Kitchen. Take a couple of coolers; one of which plugs into your lighter for travel and the wall outlet in your room for overnight. Replenish ice in plastic containers. Buy the brats, dogs, buns, and whatever else you can after you arrive in the college town. Pack things for longer travel in the middle of the van instead of the rear.

Most importantly, wear and display as many items in your school colors as possible. Take those blankets, seat cushions, hats, sweat shirts, window flags, drinking cups, napkins, towels, table linens and anything else with the school logo along with you. Enjoy!

How Colleges Treat Tailgaters

There are over a hundred division 1 and big division 1-AA schools in the United States. To get a feel for their participation in tailgating, a survey was sent to each. A total of 99 schools responded and the following data was obtained:

1. Do you allow tailgating?	100%
2. Do you encourage tailgating?	86.1%
3. Do you have parking near your stadium?	97.2%
4. Do you have non-reserved parking near your stadium?	76.4%
5. Do you reserve spaces for higher donors?	94.4%
6. Do you have toilets out in the parking areas?	75%
7. Do groups use tents, etc. for tailgate parties near stadium?	94.4%
8. Do you have fans who regularly tailgate at road games?	86.1%

The Bowl Game

Tailgating at a bowl game, can it be done? Sure, but there are a lot of questions to ask. Do you think you'll want to do it with everything else going on? Does this bowl allow parking near the stadium? Do they allow tailgating? Is the bowl site close enough for you to drive, or will you have to fly?

Start by doing your homework. Contact your school for tickets and as much information as possible. You'll need to know what events are planned for the fans from your school. Some alumni clubs plan large tent/parties where they have food service, cash bars, cheerleaders, the band, and the most logical focal point for everyone to meet. Some colleges plan pep rallies/parties the night before the game too. These one-school functions at bowl game sites are usually pretty good. Avoid the joint school parties where both bands and both sets of fans attend. These are usually just commercial functions to make money and take care of people who don't know what to do with their time.

If you need to fly to the bowl site there is still the ability to tailgate. If you are taking golf clubs you can probably pack a version of a flag pole in the bag or at least an 18 ft. ball retriever which could act as a flag pole with a little engineering (some bungee cords and duct tape). Be sure to pack window flags, a fight song tape, a folding cooler, some school color logo towels and blankets. Also pack a large flag for your motel balcony.

Make sure the vehicle you rent will suit your tailgating. It will need a tape player, room for the number of passengers you'll have and some storage. Mini vans are available from rental agencies, but they must be reserved well in advance in some cases.

The game day menu can be purchased from the deli section of a supermarket. There are sandwich meats with good breads or fried chicken available. They also have baked beans, salads of all type and great cookies for desserts. They will fix you a food or cheese tray, but try to order this the night before so you just stop in and pick it up when you leave for the game. If there are a lot of friends or people you meet at your motel who wish to participate, set up the party where everyone brings different items.

Caution: most colleges sponsor trips to their bowl games which include tickets, hotel accommodations, transportation, and some perks. These are, however, usually very expensive because they are priced up to allow a few university officials to travel free. Usually you can do much better price-wise if you purchase a private travel package or make your own reservations.

Tailgating vehicles come in four main types. There is the automobile, the station wagon, the motor home and the van (including the sport utility vehicle that looks like a van). Each of these four types has had its invention, heyday, and then its dilution of popularity by the next creation except for the van, the current vehicle of choice.

Prior to 1929, tailgaters wanting to buy a vehicle had literally hundreds of car companies from which to choose. They also had options like gas, electric or steam engines. There were, however, very few choices in styles of cars. There were box shaped cars, a few convertibles, and those little coupes with the rumble seats.

Ford introduced the country's first wagon around 1929. Although designed to take commuters to the train, it had wood sides, room for lots of people and picnic supplies, and a real tailgate. Predictably, the station wagon became the vehicle of choice for tailgating. All other major automakers followed suit eventually developing their own station wagons. For many years the wood-grained siding of the Ford Country Squire and

Tailgate Vehicle Survey

Although some schools, like BYU, have free parking and others, like California, have virtually none; stadiums throughout collegiate America generally have at least four levels of parking. There are giver lots where you don't get an admission pass unless you donate a certain amount to that school. There are also lots for smaller gift plateaus, general public lots where people pay as they arrive, and parking lots that are not part of the college stadium facility. This survey contains samples from each type of parking. It counts all vehicles (not just those being used for tailgating) parked in tailgater-frequented areas.

Cars (automobiles)	555	57%
Vans (including minis and sport utility)	367	38%
Station Wagons	30	3%
Trucks	15	1%
Motor Homes	8	1%
TOTAL	975	100%

You can drive just about anything to the game, but not all tailgating vehicles are created equal.

the Jeep Wagoneer were the "in" tailgating wagons.

Station wagons remained the prime tailgater vehicle for many years. However, beginning in the late 1940s, people who wanted more room and comfort began buying old buses and converting them into RVs. This was the catalyst which started the motor home industry. People found that they could buy a motor home and carry a large tailgate party to the game in comfort. Their group could have a bathroom, kitchen, and a place to be seen. People could drive by and see you playing cards or drinking a cocktail through the window. This was class!

Motor home industry sales and their stock prices climbed for many years, but their road peaked the last rise in the 1970s. OPEC helped create their decline with an oil embargo doubling gasoline prices almost overnight, but those who bought

motor homes had become tired of parking, fueling and storing those huge vehicles. Another problem was that the owner of this up to $60,000 investment couldn't enjoy himself. His wife refused to drive it, friends weren't experienced at this bus sized thing, so the host of the party became the designated driver. All his friends ate and drank while he drove. A less expensive, easier to drive alternative was needed. It came in the form of the passenger van.

Ford and GM tried to sell passenger vans in the 1960s, but they couldn't overcome a boxy-commercial look and rough-handling. The consumer wouldn't accept them. It took the "Hippies" with their VW Microbuses and psychedelic paint jobs to reveal the future to van makers. They put beds, chairs and TVs into their Microbuses. Cottage industries sprang up converting big vans into little motor homes. The big automakers began to see a potential in a van that was economical and easy to drive with easy chair seats and amenities like TVs and fridges.

By the early 1970s all of the Big Three auto makers were making vans which were easier to handle, more economical, and offered a cross between the motor home and a station wagon. The van became the new vehicle of choice for tailgaters because it was bigger and more comfortable than a station wagon and could be driven and operated more easily than a motor home. Vans could even be bought in school colors with accessories (like the fight song playing horn) that left no doubt for whom you were rooting.

In 1983 Lee Iacoca became head of Chrysler and saved his company. By 1985 Lee had also changed the vehicle of choice for tailgaters by bringing out the first Chrysler front wheel drive mini-van. All other US auto makers soon followed with their own mini-vans, but Chrysler sold more than the others combined. Unlike the rear wheel drive van, which still handled like a truck, this mini-van handled just as well as a car. Its front wheel drive gave it great winter traction and eliminated the need for a drive shaft. (In rear wheel drive vehicles, the hump down the center of the passenger compartment is created by the drive shaft.) There was greater interior room also and the driver sat higher from the floor than

in other vehicles. Tall or long-legged people could get in and out with ease.

Today a college stadium parking lot features all types of vehicles. Cars, station wagons, trucks and motor homes in school colors and some with window flags or bumper stickers for the home team. But the vehicle of choice for the most devoted tailgater is the van.

Buying Tailgate Transport

A tailgater's vehicle is of major importance. It must be attractive, comfortable, and give an air of school spirit. It must serve the requirements of projected tailgate parties. It must be large enough to hold guests as well as everything they "need." It can't be, however, so overbearing that it could not be used except for football Saturday.

Buying a vehicle that is too small, besides cramping everyone, causes an emotional problem as well. A cramped vehicle usually prompts the owner to plan too much. The constant checking, double-checking, fitting things into exactly the right nook and cranny usually puts pressure on the guests. This is too businesslike for a

Checklist for Buying Your Tailgate Vehicle

Your answers to the following questions will greatly assist you in your quest for the perfect tailgating vehicle.

1. How many passengers will you regularly carry to football games?

    1   2   3   4   More

	Considering tailgating equipment storage and passenger comfort, use the chart below to find the best vehicle size for your needs:					
number of passengers	*any car*	*four-door car*	*mini-van*	*long mini*	*full van*	*motor home*
one	X	X	X			
two		X	X			
three			X	X		
four				X	X	
five					X	X
more						X

2. Will the vehicle be used during the week or just for tailgating?

    Family Car   Tailgating Transport Only

If used only for tailgating transport, consult your alumni magazine for an ad for their fully loaded, school theme van. If it is to be a family car, answer below.

   2a. Do you park in a garage? What size vehicle will fit? (Length, width and height are important especially with an overhead door.) Y/N

   2b. Is gas mileage important? (Smaller vehicles generally have better EPA mileage ratings.) Y/N

   2c. Will you do icy winter driving? (Front wheel drive is great for snow and ice.) Y/N

3. Do you plan to use a radar detector or CB? (They can be built in) Y/N

4. Do you want a tape and/or CD player? (Plugs for external speakers can be built in) Y/N

5. Will you want a TV/VCR? (Can be built in at the factory.) Y/N

6. Will you want a refrigerator? (Can be done by van converter.) Y/N

7. Do you want a luggage rack? (Handy for all sorts of tailgating uses.) Y/N

football weekend. It spoils the mood. And, since tailgaters are the enterprising types, they rail at being ordered around or told that they can't bring something. It takes the spontaneous fun out of the day.

The vehicle should be large enough to handle tables, chairs, grills, coolers and whatever else the tailgater wants. There should be room in the passenger compartment for all passengers to be comfortable. People don't like to share seats with coolers or chairs. Chrysler mini-vans, for example, offer two lengths. The long vehicle has room for virtually all tailgate items behind the third seat. Their shorter version requires the passenger compartment be used for some of the hauling. Bigger full size vans not only offer better seats for passenger comfort, but they have plenty of room for tailgate supplies.

If an unusual situation arises where extra people have to be taken to a game or new items are acquired which require space, accommodations can be made. There are those rocketlike carriers (see the section on SCUDs on page 44) which attach to the luggage rack, to transport flag-poles, tarps and the like. One can also attach a standard U-Haul-type portable carrier to the roof. These external items, however, cause wind resistance, which can substantially rob the vehicle of power.

There are other space considerations too. Rubbermaid, for example, makes numerous plastic drawer-type storage bins, available with lids in school colors, which can hold non-refrigerated food and dry goods under standard mini-van seats. They also have an Action Packer to fit behind the rear seat. There are tote bags available to fit the little side wells of the vans too. Of course the tailgater must consider the measurements of all these areas before purchasing these space-saving devices.

The answer to having enough space in the vehicle isn't always to buy a huge van. A vehicle can be too large. A full-size van really takes more of everything. It needs more space to park either on the street or in a single garage stall. It takes more gas because it is heavier and less aerodynamic than a mini-van or car. It takes more driving skills too, because it turns and handles more like a truck than a car. Anyone who is considering a large vehicle should definitely drive it first. They should park it and pack it. They should answer the question, "Do I need this vehicle for other things besides the five or six football weekends per month?"

A person who plans to drive the same vehicle during the week that they use on game day will need to consider looks too. School colors are nice on Saturday, but what do they look like back home? A giant SOONERS emblazoned on the van may evoke more than school spirit, especially if you live near Austin,

Texas! Many folks use removable items which can be added to their vehicle for a game only. Window flags or spare tire covers with the school symbol are examples of such add-on items.

Tailgaters enjoy having vehicle horns which play the school fight song. Some are programmable to play other tunes too. These are great fun in the parking lot or when you pull up behind a fellow fan out on the road. This fun, however, can turn to embarrassment. Imagine a high school student being picked up by Mom, who honks the horn sending out "On Wisconsin." Your child may never speak to you again. Make sure you have a conventional horn too.

Your tailgate will need music, so make sure the vehicle has the appropriate sound system. Make sure it has a CD or cassette tape player. CDs are fine and can provide major school songs from some top flight college bands, but you can make your own tapes. You can make tapes from anything: CDs, old records and even other tapes. You can make them as long-playing as you want and repeat certain tunes as much as you want.

Seats are important in all types of vans. Be sure you sit in all the vehicle seats. Are they all comfortable enough? Do you want something fancier? Should they swivel or move up and down? Do you need them to be removable? Is there head room for tall guests?

Remember that no decision on a vehicle will answer every need. You have to take the best choice that you can afford. When the first tailgate vehicle reaches trade-in-time, buy the next one to better suit you. Obviously, a couple of years driving a vehicle makes you aware of what important features you lack.

Turtle Top Van's Weekender offers a perfect set-up for tailgating

The Right Plate

If tailgaters are going to spend so much time and money to get it all right, they would be remiss to allow their state to select their license plate for them. The correct license tag is like accessories to an expensive wardrobe. It's like sauce for a gourmet meal. It's important!

State-Sponsored Spirit Plates

Many states allow fans to purchase their college official logo plates (see above). They are slightly more expensive, but the extra money goes to support the school. And isn't your alma mater worth it?

Creative Fan Plates

There probably could be as many individually creative plates as there are tailgaters. The farther away you live from the state of your school the easier it is to get approval of your plate. For example in Minnesota I was able to get the tag "IU" for my van. In Indiana that IU tag had been taken for years. Another example would be the die-hard Kentucky fan in Idaho who has a "WILDCAT" tag on her car.

Decorative Plates

Some states don't require or even provide two license plates for vehicles. They only require a rear plate. In these states people can use front plates proclaiming their college loyalty. There are some original ideas for these tags, like "IAM 4 UK."

Favorite Parking

The following "sporting" activities are acceptable to a tailgater as long as they are done by participants who are thoughtful of their neighbors' tailgate! They are ranked in their order of popularity.

1. **Frisbee (flatball).** Generally two people, separated by 10 to 20 yards, sail a frisbee (must be in school colors) at one another enjoying both the throw for its variety and the catch for its athleticism.

2. **Football Tossing.** Generally two people (sometimes roaming bands of youth play this sport, too) separated by 10 to 20 yards throw passes to each other with a football. It is important that the throws and pass patterns be in slow-motion. The football can be a regulation-type or even a nerf ball (in school colors). There have even been reports of seat cushions, food canisters, and even plastic mustard squirters (properly closed, we hope) being used as footballs in an emergency.

3. **Topping.** This is the competition among participants in a pitch-in tailgate party to actually shock the rest of their party members. A good topper brings caviar and little toast triangles instead of their assigned chips and dip. They bring Dom Perignon instead of just "some wine." They serve a stuffed turkey instead of turkey sandwiches. They have Godiva chocolate on a silver tray instead of a bag of Hershey Miniatures. You get the idea.

4. **Flag Raising.** This contest can take weeks, months and even years to find a winner. This sport begins when one tailgater raises a new flag pole higher than their neighbor's flag. The neighboring tailgater takes up the unsaid challenge and continues the competition by finding a pole higher than the aggressor. They may buy a new pole assembly or just keep adding sections to their old pole. The competition will end when there is, or almost is, a great accident. (Like the time my assembly almost blew down in a high November wind when I flew a huge flag atop six sections, 36 feet high.) Another way the contest ends is when one participant finally pulls off the *coup de gras* and raises his flag on a helium balloon or blimp as one Indiana fan does. He reaches altitudes of over 100 feet.

Lot Sports

5. **Beer Can Stacking.** Usually done by undergraduates or younger alumni, cans are stacked when their contents have been consumed. Points are given for height, originality of stack sculpture, and engineering. Points are deducted if the stack falls or blows over in the wind. There are style points if the cans are from expensive or hard-to-find brands.

6. **Blasting.** Also usually done by undergraduates or very recent alumni. One tailgate party cranks up its music generally followed by an appropriate response from a competitor. The escalation of noise is predictable and generally makes the tailgating area uninhabitable except for undergraduates and deaf people.

7. **Bolting.** Must be planned by all (bolters) but the victim (boltee). The host/hostess usually says, "Just in case I don't get back from the john in time, here are my spare keys. Go ahead and lock up the stuff in my vehicle." After the host leaves, the rest of the guests bolt, leaving the boltee stuck with tailgate cleanup. Bolters usually just walk away to a distance where the boltee can't see them anymore. They return later when the boltee is engaged in his clean-up.

8. **Putting.** Only done by the accomplished tailgaters who has his whole tailgate so perfectly engineered that he wants a new challenge. They usually bring astroturf carpet (green), balls and putters. Wagering is common when friends from the same country club tailgate together.

9. **Keg Toss.** Similar to the hammer throw and is best when done with a spent keg from a hill or higher elevation on a grass surface. Points are given for distance and sometimes style. Warning: using a keg which still has beer may result in too much foam for future consumption.

10. **Keg Stands.** Always done by undergraduates, this is the competition of drinking beer through a hose from a keg while standing on one's head. Points are given for the length of time one can drink in this position without excessive spilling. The last time I checked the Kappa Sigs at Northwestern held the championship title.

Tents, Tarps and Shelters

Looking across a college football parking lot you see a moving panorama of brightly colored flags snapping in the wind, smoke rising from grills, vehicles parking, airborne footballs and frisbees, and usually some large colorful tents. These tents are logically used to provide cover from rain or sun. But, more often than not, they are also used to make a statement or to identify a special group's gathering place for entertainment.

Tents have a rich history dating back to biblical times when they were used to shelter nomadic tribes. Today, colorful tents appear at all kinds of outdoor affairs. Events like fairs, horse races, tennis tournaments, and garden weddings utilize tents. Big time golf tournaments always allow for sponsor tents. Lately, college football is beginning to sprout its share of these colorful canvas canopies.

Our survey of colleges shows (see page 17) that 94.4% of the schools rent tents or tent space to special groups in their tailgating areas. These are groups like booster clubs, fraternities and alumni clubs. Commercial groups also rent tents to promote their products.

Real tailgaters, people who religiously picnic from their vehicles, don't patronize the big entertainment tents. This is because they don't like

Our Academy Broadway Gazebo

football fans in suits and ties, institutional food, cash bars, and people who don't take college football seriously. It is permitted, however, for a tailgater to attend the festivities at one of the large tents in two situations; the first is homecoming. A tailgater may want to go to his or her fraternity/sorority tent to see old classmates who are in from out of state for one game a year. The second case for attending a tent festivity is if the tailgater is to receive an award from a club which is hosting a tent party, he (or she) is allowed to attend the ceremony, shake hands and leave. The real tailgater will always, however, return to his or her own vehicle after the game to resume their picnicking.

In spite of their disdain for big entertainment tents, tailgaters will use smaller versions, tarps or other type shelters. These covers are a great way to allow a party to continue even if it's raining. They also prevent sunburn when used in early season games (before November in the South and before August in Minnesota).

In recent years there has been a boom in the portable shelter industry. For little more than a hundred dollars a tailgater can now own an easy to assemble Academy Broadway "Gazebo" tent which covers an area of 10.5 by 10.5 feet. These colorful little versions of the entertainment tent fold away into a little bag that easily fits under a mini van's seats or in a roof top SCUD (see page 44). The Gazebo can be setup on a hard surface as well as on grass so it is doubly useful to tailgaters. There are also colorful tarps and bungee cords available at any discount or hardware store to use in making shelters too. A little engineering and experimentation can take you a long way in constructing your ideal shelter.

If you keep in mind that people shouldn't tailgate when it is extremely cold, windy or rainy, tents can be made for all other circumstances. Two vans parked eight to twelve feet apart can hold a stretched tarp between them. Bungee cords can anchor the corners of the tarp to the luggage racks to provide stability. Use a PVC pole to hold up the center and the tarp becomes a simple tent!

Variations of the above tent will generally evolve through trial and error. A grommet can be made for the center of the tarp to hold the tent pole and prevent tearing the material. Three PVC poles can be made to fit together to provide a long center support for the tent. The tent builders can make their shelter deeper by using four vans for its corners.

Probably the most ambitious undertaking, however, is for a tailgater with only one van to make a vehicle anchored tent. However, with the right equipment, a side canopy is quite easy and works almost as well as a full tent. The canopy requires a

WARNING   DO NOT MAKE THIS TENT IN THE WIND

EYE BOLTS TO FASTEN TARP

PVC FRAME
TO HOLD TARP
AWAY FROM
VEHICLE

COMMON DISCOUNT STORE TARP

OVER LUGGAGE RACK

UNDER LUGGAGE RACK

PVC POLE
WITH EYE BOLT
EVEN WITH WHEEL
TO FASTEN TARP

STEEL OR PLYWOOD RECTANGLES

"L" BRACKETS
WITH BOLT &
WING NUTS

few extra pieces of equipment. There must be parking plates. These are simple sheets of steel that have anchors built in for the tent poles. By driving over the plates, the van driver makes the base of the tent stable. A large PVC "U" is bolted to the plates by its open ends with simple finger turned wing nuts. The tent canopy is completed by hooking a tarp to the vehicle luggage rack with the other side hooked to the loop part of the "U" with hook type bolts. A word of caution, however; if there is any wind, the canopy will need to be stabilized with a bungee cord to a heavy cooler or milk jug full of water, or your tent will be "gone with the wind."

Where's Johnny?

Considering that the average drive to a game is two drinks long and the first thing served in the parking lot is another drink, toilets, or the lack of toilets, are a concern to the tailgater. Our survey of schools shows that 75% of the colleges in America have decided to provide some sort of facilities in their parking area for the tailgaters. Wisconsin has small parking areas next to buildings which have open rest rooms on game days. Illinois, Indiana and many others have rows of little plastic outhouses. Arizona opens its basketball arena with their rest rooms.

In the old days, five years ago, colleges didn't worry about toilets for tailgaters. The fan had to either refrain from the consumption of any liquids or make a pit stop just prior to entering the stadium lots. Then fans would exercise moderation in their consumption of liquids until time to enter the stadium. The poor gas station or McDonalds nearest the main route to the stadium probably had an extremely high water bill in the Fall.

Tailgaters, being great problem solvers, have invented their own portable toilet facilities. The camping industry has sold portable toilets for years. They can be purchased at discount stores as well as sporting goods outlets. They range from inexpensive to elaborate, but most importantly, they are small enough to fit safely, without spill or smell, into a packed van. The only problem is modesty.

To solve this dilemma try the idea on the next page. A simple PVC "U" attached to a luggage rack can act as a curtain rod. An opaque shower curtain or tarp with shower hooks

Joy's Johns at Notre Dame: they're not beautiful until after that third drink is consumed

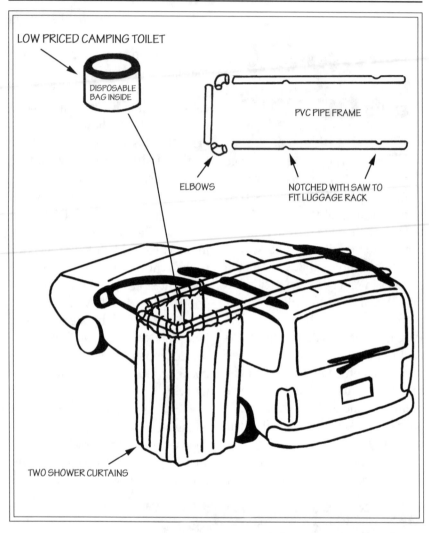

LOW PRICED CAMPING TOILET

DISPOSABLE
BAG INSIDE

PVC PIPE FRAME

ELBOWS

NOTCHED WITH SAW TO
FIT LUGGAGE RACK

TWO SHOWER CURTAINS

attached will give the desired privacy from three sides. In our test model, we hooked a large wet towel into the van window on the fourth side not only for privacy but as a place to clean your hands.

Problem: Where do you empty it after the trip?

Solution: Some of these toilets have a plastic bag liner for easy disposal at the first rest area on the way home. You can simply empty the bag in a toilet and flush; however, be careful that the odor fighting liquid you use in your portable toilet is one that won't damage the septic system.

Throwing TP at Games

Toilet paper or tissue, as it's called on TV, is an important item to carry to college football games. It can be purchased by the roll, or in quantities of four, eight, 12, 24 or 48 rolls. It can be "borrowed" from a motel, if your game trip happens to be an over-nighter. Or, if you are an undergraduate you may liberate it from the toilets in the dorm or other campus buildings.

Although there are generally three colors and several prints available in toilet paper, plain white is the only acceptable kind. Only fans of Columbia and North Carolina can throw the powder blue rolls without raising eye brows. To date no one has ever thrown pink. Undergraduates sometimes throw paper towel rolls, but this can be dangerous. The extra weight and long design of towel rolls may cause injury to your arm unless your throw has been practiced. Also, the paper towel's streamer is too wide and heavy to make an attractive flutter when tossed.

Ten Good Reasons
you should take t.p.
to college football games:

10. It's fun to throw and watch that long white stream after a score by your team

9. Long white streamers always improve the ambiance at a large gathering

8. It's a gift from above that keeps on giving as it's re-thrown until gone or on the field

7. Spent streamers of it can be bunched up to keep your feet warm on a cold day

6. You can be Johnny on the spot if your date comes back to her seat and says "Rats, they're out again in the rest room."

5. It acts as an inconspicuous cover in a bag containing a hidden stash of beer or a whiskey bottle

4. If your aim is good it will bother opposing school fans who have no right to be sitting closer to the field than you

3. Throwing is a good exercise to burn those extra tailgating calories

2. It can be traded for beer to tailgaters with stomach problems

1. Throwing it really bothers tree huggers

Take a Load Off

OFFICIAL TAIL...

The station wagon tailgate, once the mainstay of the pregame picnic, has been replaced as the table of choice for tailgaters. This is because there are no longer very many station wagons and vans don't have gates that fold out and down. Van gates fold up, making a small roof, or they have side hinged doors. Today's tailgaters have to pack tables to take along for food service.

There are many varieties of tables found in a stadium parking lot. There are the small four seat portable picnic variety, card tables and larger, aluminum models. Now, there are also modern space age resin tables being used for tailgating. However, there are some clearly superior products on the market.

Folding picnic tables by Academy Broadway are nifty and inexpensive (around $60). They are sold at discount stores and camping equipment outlets. Light and sturdy, the tables' greatest attribute, however, is that they fold into a 15 by 34" plastic rectangle with carrying handles. They fit under or behind mini-van seats or in a car trunk. These tables have four corner seats (11x12") and a top

Our normal game day set-up fits and packs easily into our minivan

(34x26") made of colorful green plastic resin. Their legs are stainless steel.

Another good choice would be plastic resin tables like those from Syroco, the industry leader. Most consist of a top and four removable legs. They come in different colors and shapes and are evolving to give more utility and better esthetic qualities every year. They even come with umbrellas. They clean up with a wet rag and, since they are impervious to elements in the air or rain, can be left out on the patio year round. They are sturdy enough to hold hundreds of pounds. The top, with its reinforcing, is less than an inch thick and the disassembled legs fit under mini-van seats. These tables are inexpensive and available at discount stores or anywhere there is lawn furniture.

Once you have a place to put your food, the next step is to have a comfortable chair. The old standby, aluminum folding chairs with the web strapped seats are being replaced as the chairs of choice. They bend and break under the weight of large men and they blow around in the wind. Today's tailgater is making much use of either the director's chair or plastic resin seats. They hold up better and last longer.

A classic director's chair can be bought with a wooden or metal frame and canvas to match school colors. The canvas can be lettered at a sign shop with a name or school logo.

They fold to a very small package and will hold a big load comfortably. The canvas can be replaced in an instant too. Director's chairs can be bought from department stores.

Plastic resin chairs and little end tables are available again from companies like Syroco in the same stores as the big tables. Some of them fold while the others can be stacked. Don't shy away from stacking four to six chairs. They fit nicely, upside down, in one mini-van seat. And these chairs just may be the strongest and most comfortable seats in the parking lot. They last forever!

Staying "Cool"

Portable ice chests, or "coolers" to today's tailgaters, got their start relatively recently with Igloo, the premier manufacturer in the cooler industry, which was not even founded until 1947. But, like many products produced today, the materials of the space age have made it possible for coolers to be much more effective at a more reasonable cost. Ice chests began as costly heavy steel galvanized affairs with metal latches but have become brightly colored, lightweight, low-cost plastic. There are even folding and "disposable" models.

When planning to buy an ice chest, a tailgater needs to consider performance (the ability to keep things cold) and durability. There have been very few published comparisons of domestic coolers; however, in the September 1992 issue of *Boating* magazine, B. Fedorko found that the Igloo 54 quart chest outperformed (its ice lasted longest) similar sized coolers from Coleman and Rubbermaid. Channel 12, KPNX, in Phoenix, also ran a 36 hour summer test on the roof of a downtown building in 1994. Once again Igloo won. Finally, John Penton released a 1990 study from the University of Houston comparing these domestic "big three." Penton's tests found Rubbermaid and Igloo virtually even in performance, but that Igloo was the most consistent. These Igloo models claim to support up to 300 pounds of weight (remember the old commercial with the jeep sitting atop four igloo 48 qt. ice chests?). That should be enough proof for even the most skeptical tailgater!

Consumer Reports compared types of coolers in their 1990 Buying Guide and proved that insulated coolers are superior to non-insulated models (the foam boxes) because the insulated models have several layers which work better than foam alone. They also found that smaller coolers can make a limited supply of ice last

longer, but a larger model can stay cold longer because it can hold much more ice. Their annual *Buyer's Guides* also periodically compares cooler values by manufacturer.

Consumer's Ice Melt Test

Inside temp 32/outside temp 100

Quart Size	Ice Melt (per hour)
89	1.8 lbs
45	1.1 lbs
35	.8 lbs
15.5	5 oz

Or if you're an engineering grad from Purdue, MIT or Georgia Tech, use Penton's "easy" formula to compare heat loss to claimed volume. This formula is:

Q=-54.829 + 47.477 log(v)

Space is also an important consideration when buying coolers. How much room is available in your vehicle? It is best if the tailgater measures the space between and behind seats in their vehicle to compare with prospective cooler dimensions. A huge cooler which can't be lifted when full and is too big to allow the van gate to be shut is useless on game day. Take your vehicle along when shopping and try different coolers in the space you have.

Owning more than one cooler is probably a wise idea for a serious

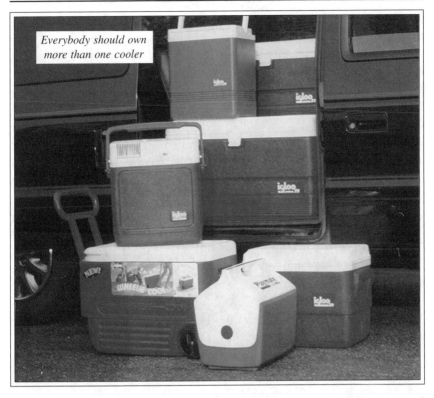

Everybody should own more than one cooler

tailgater for several reasons. First, two or three smaller coolers are always easier to load and unload and fit into your vehicle than a huge chest. Second, food and drinks should be kept separate. Foods need more care and protection against airborne dirt and bacteria than drinks do. The drink cooler will be constantly opened and shut, but the food will be dispensed only once or twice during the tailgate. No need to expose the foods too often. Finally, make sure to pack a small cooler for the passenger compartment to serve snacks and cold beverages to travelers on the trips to and from the game.

Coolers come in all sizes and shapes. We've tried models that hold a great quantity of items (72 quarts) and some that hold only a couple of sandwiches and a drink. There are models that hold upright two liter bottles and those that have wheels. We even tested a model that plugs into the vehicle's cigarette lighter or a wall outlet. It heats as well as cools, although not at the same time. Some coolers, like the Igloo Playmate, have their own ice source; it's called a canteen and can be frozen and placed back into the cooler.

A word about ice or cooling matter. We've found that a plastic milk jug that is cleaned out, filled not quite to the brim with water and frozen the night before a game works just as well, if not better than, store-bought ice bags or expensive freezer packs. However, if you are itching for the latest innovation in ice box cooling equipment, Igloo makes ice bottles and freeze flasks that accomplish basically the same task as the milk jug except that they are sturdier and come in special sizes to fit between cans and bottles better. The ice in these jugs lasts all day and will provide a little drinking or hand washing water as it melts, too.

If you would like to have ice cubes for your drinks, you can raid your ice maker the morning of the game for cubes and fill a large Rubbermaid Serv 'n Save canister. These cubes melt faster than the jug ice, but when packed in the cooler with the jug ice they help keep the cooler cold and are zero trouble to pack up when empty.

Another innovation is for drinks that get warm before tailgaters finish them. This handy individual cooler is called "The Fridge" and it allows you to have your beverage constantly surrounded by ice while you are enjoying periodic drinks. The Fridge is the size of a regular can, glass or bottle size (there is some flexibility for slightly larger or smaller drink vessels). Prior to a tailgate party all you do is freeze it. Its blue gel gets colder than regular ice. So while tailgaters consume their beverages, their drinks actually get colder. The Fridge's insulated exterior comes in several designs and sometimes is available in school logos.

There are even individual drink coolers

The Tailgater's Friend

The stadium parking lot, on Football Saturday, is the scene of tens of thousands of neat fans, thousands of interesting tailgate vehicles, hundreds of multifamily super tailgate parties and scores of colorful flags. There may be, however, only a few really special pieces of tailgating equipment seen throughout this whole gathering. Equipment that is so unique, it draws its own crowd; like the buffalo shaped grill that is towed by a van to Colorado games or a school flag attached to a helium blimp that floats hundreds of feet above the Indiana parking lot. I have one such special item: the Coleman Kitchen.

The Coleman Kitchen is a table, counter, utensil rack, towel holder, sink with a real drain, game board and suitcase "all-in-one." This kitchen is amazingly well built. It comes as a case which, when folded, is only 7½ inches thick, 42 inches long and 21¾ inches high. Its weight is 35 lbs. It has a handle for easy carrying and a cover similar to some sporting goods. It has stainless steel construction where it needs strength: counter tops, frame and legs. It is plastic where it needs color or things have the potential to be removed like the sink and game top. The latches and leg catches are steel and absolutely first-class.

My Coleman kitchen is like a magnet. It draws people from nearby parking spaces and makes people

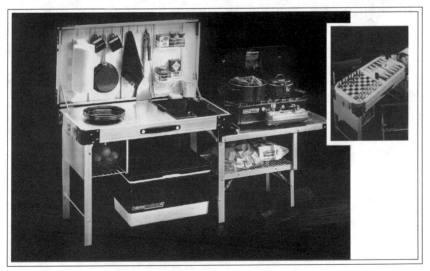

walking through take the time to stop and look. I take it out of the back of the mini-van, unzip its case, unsnap the catches, unfold it and, voila, there's a one piece kitchen! People casually watch while it's being setup. You can see their eyes follow my moves and read their lips as they call attention to it; "Hey look at this!" When my tailgate is in full swing with foods being cooked and served from the Coleman, people also drop by to check it out and the usual response is, "What is this?" or "Boy is that neat!" Next thing you know, introductions have been made and anecdotes are being shared about camping or tailgating experiences.

At the '93 Freedom Bowl, my tailgate was given the prime reserved position, outside the main entrance to the stadium. The TV stations were told that *The Tailgater's Handbook* tailgate was to be set up out in the parking lot. All the stations visited the setup. There were two from Louisville, one from the Shreveport station and one from the Freedom Bowl Network came by. Three of the four TV crews used artsy openings panning away from Brats cooking on a grill sitting on the Coleman. The fourth ended with a complete tour of the ideal tailgate "kitchen."

> If you tailgate, you
> need a Coleman Kitchen!

Food Storage

This book is full of references to serve and save containers. But what do you look for in a good tailgating container?

Food containers for tailgating must be simple. They must hold your food, close/seal easily, stand up to rough handling, be dishwasher safe, and look nice for serving. They also need to be easily stored during the week and the off season.

Many foods already come in reusable containers. There are plastic mustard squirter/bottles which can be used for Mayo, Barbecue sauce, water or your own blend. They hold up fairly well over the year and most now have screw off lids which are easy to operate. Deli items, like pasta or macaroni salads usually come in plastic "reusable" containers, but these packages are too flimsy to keep for the long run. If you don't want to hand wash and carefully store them, these containers will cause you less frustration if you throw them into your recycling after you return home from the game. Some ice creams are sold in gallon or half gallon plastic

Container "Can't-Do-Withouts"

• Square set of containers, each progressively larger than the last, that store inside each other. The largest container is about nine inches square and less than four inches thick. Great for sliced onions, pickles, dips, foods in smaller quantities and leftovers. The larger containers are perfect for salads.

• Rectangle-shaped set of containers that also store inside one another. The larger container is approximately 13 inches on its long side.These rectangle-shaped containers are great for meat loaf, banana nut bread, bread, sliced buns, precooked brats, hot dogs, cookies, salads or leftovers.

• Canister shaped containers that again store inside one another, the largest being eight inches on every side. These are great for large or small pasta salads, potato salads and as ice containers. They can also be filled with chili and frozen.

• Dip & Snack and Party Food Trays are also perfect for tailgating. Each is separated into compartments with a dip section in the center. They also have the famous sealing lid. Perfect for veggies and dip, fruits, cheeses and hors d'oeuvres.

buckets which are good for reuse a few times if you are careful. They are good for freezing chili or soup the night before and then for transporting it to the tailgate. You don't care what they look like because the contents are served from a pot, not the plastic container with all those partial words in differing stages of wear.

To save frustration on game day, we recommend that tailgaters consider the following containers:

1. Everyone needs several plastic mustard bottles, of which one should still contain mustard. The others should be sterilized in the dishwasher and used for liquid condiments which don't come in squeeze bottles. You can write on the side of these bottles with a marker or you can buy condiment bottles that are made of see-through, heavy-duty plastic.

These fit inside each other for easy storage

2. Everyone needs an assortment of Rubbermaid Servin' Saver square corner food containers. Use only the square or rectangle shaped containers to conserve space in your food cooler. We also recommend multiple sizes of each shape when possible. All of the Servin' Saver containers are made of heavy-duty

plastic with pliable, easy-to-seal lids that keep food airtight. They now offer EZ Topps containers too which can be operated by people with arthritis or even small children. They are dishwasher safe and have some color choices. The best part is that you can find these containers in discount stores at very low prices.

These are perfect for dips and veggies

3. You also should have an Action Packer plastic storage container. They are to hold all paper goods, table cloths, towels, cutlery and even nonperishable foods. They keep everything dry and even act as a seat for two people. These waterproof containers are made of reinforced, heavy-duty plastic with snap-shut, lockable handles. Be sure to measure the area available behind the last seat in your mini-van to select the appropriate size from the available choices. You might find that you want to keep your Action Packer in the mini-van permanently because they are great, light storage chests that keep items from sliding around in the rear of the van.

Grills and Stoves

Most real tailgaters aren't into sushi and health food. They are more the bratwurst type. They like barbecued chicken and hearty meat sandwiches with peppers, onions and mustard. Sure they'll eat a little caviar, if someone else brings it, but the only way they would touch most raw fish is if they were going to throw it during the game. So you need to plan on how you're going to cook the burgers.

Grills can be used for both barbecuing and heating. That's right, they do a great job heating a pot of chili as well as cooking brats. They range in price from a couple of dollars to thousands. There are all sizes of grills too. Some tailgaters tow their grills just like a boat and others can put them in paper bags under a van seat.

When deciding what grill to purchase, tailgaters have three considerations. They need to look at the amount of grill surface they want, the amount of vehicle transport space they have, and the type of fuel they want to use.

Our Coleman stove and Char-Broil portable grill with gas — the grill's twin works with charcoal.

How much grill surface you will need is determined somewhat by the menu and the party. If you are planing on cooking a lot of meats that need to be done at the same time (steaks) or if you are cooking for a large group that doesn't want to eat in shifts, you will need more grilling space. You will also need more surface if you want some space to heat other foods or cook a second choice of main course.

Surface space of a grill can also be determined by your storage space. What kind of space is available in the vehicle to transport this cooker? If space is never a problem, some people bring large grills like you see on a deck in the suburbs. However, most people have to compromise and find a size which will pack well in their vehicle. It is generally better for larger groups to have the flexibility of several small grills rather than one hard to handle large cooker. The most common grill found in stadium parking lots is Char-Broil's Table Top Gas or Charcoal model. It is very small and has foldable legs.

The fuel of choice is charcoal for picnickers who have a preference for foods with an open pit flavor. Foods like steak and hamburgers just seem to taste better when cooked over coals. Here the decision is between regular briquettes with starter fluid or Match Light instant lighting charcoal briquetts from Kingsford. Match Light is by far the most popular among tailgaters because it's so simple to use. All you have to do is light the briquettes and in minutes you can be cooking. Anything that saves time and space is a must for tailgating.

The second fuel choice is gas. We invariably use our Char-Broil Table Top gas model. It grills as soon as we light it and has an adjustable flame. Its very inexpensive fuel is available at any discount store in those little canisters people use with plumbing torches or similar, fatter, camping models. We've also learned to always have a full backup fuel container because it is hard to judge how much fuel is left in a used canister.

If your tailgating menu includes foods you'll need to fry in a pan or cook in a pot you ought to invest in a good, portable camping stove. Foods can be warmed on a grill, but the heat concentration necessary to fry eggs, pancakes or fish just isn't right. Some tailgaters also like to prepare large pots of soup or chili which are often well chilled or frozen. These heat must faster on a stove.

When tailgaters unpack their stoves, they are almost always made by Coleman. After all, Coleman has about 90% of the camping stove market. They make stoves which operate with propane and those that use liquid fuel. We use a two-burner dual fuel stove. It operates on either Coleman fuel or less expensive unleaded gasoline. It isn't a grill because it has burners just like a kitchen stove. These burners are built to resist wind and there are three folding sides which provide more protection from wind.

Roof Rockets

Ever see a vehicle moving down the highway with what looks like a rocket attached to the roof? It's weird! People stare and holler. They all point and make sure all their passengers see it too. These "rockets" can be seen in a variety of school colors and often have graphics on them proclaiming loyalties " Go Big Red" or "Beat State." No matter how colorful or striking they appear, however, these roof rockets don't actually propel anything!

These odd looking tubes are aerodynamic cargo carriers made of large plastic pipe (PVC). They are used to carry items like artificial grass rugs, flag poles, braces, tent poles and tarps that are too long or large to fit into the passenger section of the vehicle. Our rocket began its maiden voyage just after the 1990 Gulf War so we named it the "IU SCUD."

SCUDs can be made in any size or length that will fit on your vehicle's roof. Plan your tube so that it will hold the longest item that you will have to pack. PVC pipes come in any diameter, but 6 to 10-inch diameters work best for SCUD building. The larger pipes, ten inch diameter for example, come in lengths longer than a SCUD so they will have to be cut. PVC pipe can be cut, sawed, drilled and worked much like wood. So use a hand saw to cut it to size.

After cutting the PVC, you will need to have a cover for the front and a door for the rear. The same place that sells you the pipe will sell you a cap which can be used as a front cover. Or you can purchase a fiberglass cone to serve the same purpose and give better driving aerodynamics. These nose cones and caps can be permanently cemented to the SCUD. The rear door can be made easily from a piece of plywood. Cut the wood into a disk to fit the interior of the opening. You can then fasten it to the roof rocket with thumbscrews or small padlocks.

Now there has to be something which attaches the SCUD to the luggage rack. Tie-down straps for cargo hauling will work, but the rocket can shift back and forth when the vehicle accelerates and decelerates. Our stability solution was to add small "L" shaped brackets onto the bottom of the SCUD, which were spaced apart the width of the luggage rack cross pieces. When these brackets fit down over the cross pieces of the rack, the movement stopped. Luggage racks also have small adjustable pieces which can be slid in and tightened against the sides of the SCUD to prevent the rocket from moving right or left. To prevent the SCUD from bouncing up and down we added a bolt between the rear "L" brackets which anchored everything. For security purposes, a bicycle lock was substituted for the bolt on the front brackets.

The greatest problem for SCUD builders is painting it. PVC doesn't have a porous surface to which paint will readily adhere. If you sand the surface, paint will hold better or you can purchase a liquid which reacts

Our first roof rocket, circa 1990

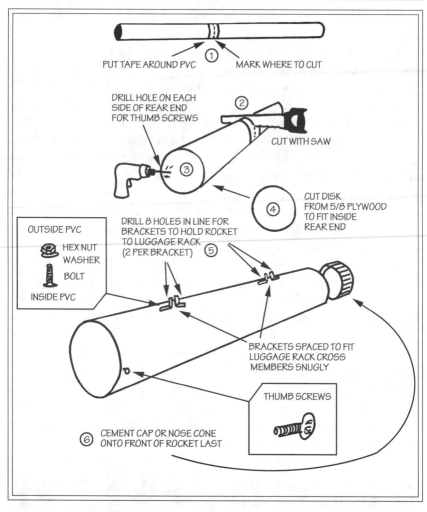

PUT TAPE AROUND PVC   ①   MARK WHERE TO CUT

DRILL HOLE ON EACH SIDE OF REAR END FOR THUMB SCREWS

② CUT WITH SAW

③

④ CUT DISK FROM 5/8 PLYWOOD TO FIT INSIDE REAR END

OUTSIDE PVC

HEX NUT
WASHER
BOLT

INSIDE PVC

DRILL 8 HOLES IN LINE FOR BRACKETS TO HOLD ROCKET TO LUGGAGE RACK (2 PER BRACKET) ⑤

BRACKETS SPACED TO FIT LUGGAGE RACK CROSS MEMBERS SNUGLY

THUMB SCREWS

⑥ CEMENT CAP OR NOSE CONE ONTO FRONT OF ROCKET LAST

with the PVC to make a paintable surface. These are difficult or expensive treatments.

Our test SCUD was only painted at the nose cap and rear door. We used cheap red spray paint from a discount store spraying several coats and keeping the remainder of the can for touch ups. The paint held for years. Since my school colors are red and

white (Indiana) the white glossy body of the SCUD was an ideal place for red graphics. We put four inch red vinyl letters spelling "INDIANA HOOSIERS" on one side and "BEAT THE" on the other. Each week we change the name of our opponent so that the SCUD is ready for the game.

The letters come in some choice of colors and can be picked up at discount office marts. They are peel and stick vinyl so just press them onto the PVC. Later we added white letters making the words "IU SCUD" to the front cap. The lettering looked professional and drew double takes on the highway.

Flags, Poles and Bases

What college football stadium parking lot would be complete without a number of colorful flags proclaiming school loyalty against a blue sky? And what loyal fan would be without a flag for his vehicle or to wave after touchdowns during the game? The problem: where do you get them and how do you properly display them once they are in your possession?

Flags can be purchased just about anywhere you find officially licensed school merchandise. The stadium spirit shop or school book store will have flags imprinted with the school or team logo. They may even have a few variations from which to choose. Many sporting goods stores will sell college flags as do the licensed logo shops that are in every mall. State flags can be purchased from flag companies. Or you can even have flags made to your specifications by the numerous flag printing outfits that are usually listed in the yellow pages. If you want something derogatory like "Screw Purdue" or Muck Fichigan" you'll probably need to have it made.

The hardest part about flying a flag, however, isn't buying one, it's developing a suitable pole and stand. A flag, depending on its size and weight, exerts a tremendous amount of pressure against its pole and base, even in a mere 10 mph wind. The longer the pole, the greater the leverage of the wind. So tailgaters will have to decide what kind of a statement is their flag going to make and does it have to fly higher than all the others?

If you want to have the highest flying flag, remember it's just like money, someone always has more of it. At Indiana it's escalated so much that one fan eventually began to raise his flag on a cable attached to a small red and white helium blimp. He has reached well over 100 feet of altitude.

Professional flag companies will sell flag pole sets that come in sections. There are normally three six-foot sections to make an 18-foot pole. You can add an extra sections in some cases, but using too many can be a hazard in high winds. These companies appear at home shows and can be found in the yellow pages. A local cemetery or a veteran's

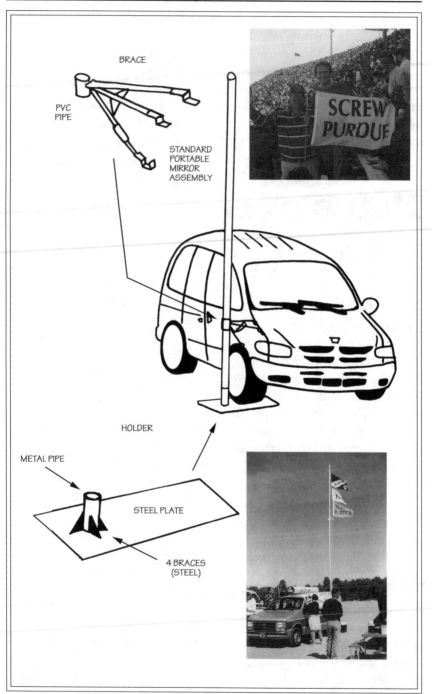

BRACE

PVC PIPE

STANDARD PORTABLE MIRROR ASSEMBLY

SCREW PURDUE

HOLDER

METAL PIPE

STEEL PLATE

4 BRACES (STEEL)

organization should have a catalog from a good flag company.

Once the height of the flag pole is decided, the stand or base has to be engineered. Always find a way to anchor the flag set to your vehicle. Most people have a stand made which has a holder for the pole and enough extra base that they can drive over it with a van wheel. The van holds the stand in place and a brace higher up the pole provides the final stability to fly the flags in all types of wind. The brace can be a "T" made of PVC pipe attached to the luggage rack or it can be more elaborate. An extension mirror assembly (used to add a mirror to a vehicle so they may haul large trailers) has been found to be of value to tailgaters. This assembly fits under the hood and the fender. It has a turn buckle which can tighten the contraption to the van. We replaced the mirror with a piece of PVC slightly larger in diameter than the flag poles. It works well and is very easy to put on quickly.

Flags to be taken into the stadium have a simple common problem. The pole to fly them has to be carried into the stadium and stored between touchdowns. The longer the pole, the harder it is to store. The best solution is a golf ball retriever. It is made of light weight aluminum and telescopes to a length of 18 feet. They have PVC ends that can be drilled to hold a snap or ring for the top of the flag. The bottom sliding ring of your flag should be of a heavy metal so it will hold the bottom of the flag down just through gravity. Ball retrievers do lose their tightness through frequent use, and they will collapse unless the flag waver uses flags made of lightweight material.

The Best Band in the Land

Since 1982 the John Philip Sousa Foundation presents the Sudler Award to the best collegiate marching band in America. And the winners are:

1995 Purdue   1988 Michigan State

1994 James Madison   1987 Oklahoma

1993 UCLA   1986 Texas

1992 Northwestern   1985 Florida A&M

1991 Arizona State   1984 Ohio State

1990 Iowa   1983 Illinois

1989 Kansas   1982 Michigan

Purdue's "All-American" Marching Band

Rock the House

OFFICIAL TAILGATER

The art of tailgating requires a certain amount of atmosphere that can only be achieved with the appropriate music. How better to get excited than to hear a few renditions of the fight song while watching the flags on the stadium flap in the breeze? What better way to end a winning day at the stadium than a rendition of the alma mater as the sun drops in the autumn sky across an almost empty parking lot? And what better way to make a statement to some opposing fan when you are still some 50 miles from the stadium than the fight song played on a hidden speaker as you drive by.

Sound systems are simple. They consist of a tape player, the music you like on tape, and speakers where you can hear the results. They can be as simple as a boom box that you set on a table or as elaborate as speakers attached to the luggage rack.

Tailgate professionals make their own tapes. They dub from their school marching band's most recent tape or CD version of their school fight songs and alma mater. There is an art to building excitement on the game day tape. You must begin with gentle and then progress to faster music with repetitions of key tunes. You might even add in opposing fight songs and other famous marches. Some use steam train sounds, antiaircraft guns, play-by-play recordings from great victories and music by artists they like. Just make sure that you use a nice long-playing tape. You don't want to have to get up every 30 minutes to turn the tape over.

Notre Dame seniors play one last victory march

The Greatest College Fight Songs

1. Notre Dame Victory March

This is probably the second most played tune in America after *The Star Spangled Banner*.

2. On Wisconsin

The fight song of 40% of the high schools in the country (the 40% that don't use Notre Dame's fight song).

3. Illinois Loyalty

This is actually two fight songs in one. The first tune is very familiar; the second is also familiar, but not always with the first half attached.

4. The Victors (Michigan)

Rousing and easy to sing, this song's roots go back to the days when Stagg coached rival Chicago.

5. Rise Northwestern

This is a peppy, after-touchdown song that gets fans excited. It's actually their backup fight song.

6. Go You Northwestern

The Wildcats' traditional fight song has a great melody.

7. Buckeye Battle Cry (Ohio State)

This is a peppy, backup fight song which makes up for their gentle primary fight song.

8. Minnesota Rouser

This one will bring you to your feet except when played in a Teflon dome. It is frequently copied by high schools.

9. Fight, Tiger (Missouri)

Its melody will fire up a pep rally. It flows so well you know what notes follow.

10. Maine Stein Song

This is a great melody with a history that dates back to tweeds and libraries with fireplaces.

The Next Ten:

11. Down the Field (Yale)
12. Nittany Lion (Penn State)
13. Down, Down the Field (Syracuse)
14. Princeton Cannon Song
15. Hail Purdue

16. MSU Fight (Michigan State)
17. Dear Old Nebraska U
18. Roll On, Tulane
19. Fight On, Pennsylvania
20. Roar, Lion, Roar (Columbia)

A Few More Great Fight Songs...

Across the Field (Ohio State)
Anchors Aweigh (Navy)
Bow Down to Washington
Bula, Bula (Yale)
Fight on USC (Southern California)

Indiana, Our Indiana
Iowa Fight Song
On Brave Old Army Team
Rambling Wreck from Georgia Tech
Washington and Lee Swing

The Commandments

1. **Thou shalt not make others tailgate.**
   No matter how dedicated you are, most other people don't like to tailgate in rain, cold or otherwise foul weather. Don't force them to tailgate.

2. **Thou shalt not arrive at the last minute.**
   Never rush. Always arrive early. You are, however, permitted to rush your spouse and family while at home if they are preventing you from being early.

3. **Thou shalt park where lot security guards are discreet.**
   Parking lot employees must be reasonable or, at least, bribable. Find a lot where they are. Offensive employees are fair game for wide turns, practical jokes, etc.

4. **Thou shalt always park in the same place.**
   Find an ideal parking space and keep it forever.

5. **Thou shalt always use thy vehicle as an anchor.**
   Use your vehicle as an anchor for tents, tarps, flag poles or equipment vulnerable to wind. Items like luggage racks and trailer hitches make great additions to this anchor.

6. **Thou shalt have a designated driver.**

7. **Thou shalt improve thy tailgate every week.**
   Every activity you repeat, week to week, must be improved upon continually.

8. **Thou shalt not be a cheapskate.**
   It is considered in poor taste for a person shopping for tailgate foods and beverages to mention the word "budget." If a budget must be followed, do so in a reticent manner. It is acceptable, even when on a budget, to purchase the more expensive brands of labeled alcoholic beverages because you want the best for your family and friends.

9. **Thou shalt not be found without fuel.**
   If you cook with gas, always have a back-up full fuel container in your vehicle (just in case).

# of Tailgating

10. **Thou shalt have plenty.**
    Never run out of food or drink. It is better to have too much than not enough.

11. **Thou shalt not diet.**
    Diets must be forgotten on game day. Pistachio ice cream, guacamole, and green pasta may be considered "greens" by real tailgaters.

12. **Thy tailgate party shall have only *one* chef.**

13. **Thou shalt dress appropriately.**
    Tailgaters must buy and wear traditionally styled clothes that tend to be expensive, cut generously, made from natural fibers, and last for more than one season. These clothes may only be replaced when they wear out and can no longer be repaired. No neckties at tailgates, please!

14. **Thou shalt not endorse the NFL at thy tailgate.**
    Do not wear any item of clothing which is an officially licensed product of the NFL. If you want to wear that stuff, tailgate on Sunday in front of the TV.

15. **Thou shalt not resist progress.**
    Any invention that works better, faster and saves space must eventually be purchased.

16. **Thou shalt not talk politics.**
    Politics are to be avoided at a tailgate party. If your guests persist in bringing up politics, animal rights or gun control, you are permitted to demonstrate a reason for gun control.

17. **Thou shalt not assault the eardrums of thy neighbors.**
    Do not play loud music in the parking/picnicking area. The only acceptable music is of the fight song variety, and it must be kept at a reasonable level.

18. **Thou shalt not depart the stadium parking lot for home before the traffic has cleared.**

Have a Drink?

C ollege tailgating could be compared to a cocktail party. It is a mixture of men and women fans drinking alcoholic beverages like cocktails, beer and wine and nonalcoholic things like coffee, pop and bottled water. Not everyone drinks alcohol, yet they mingle with people who do. There are snacks and hors d'oeuvres to munch, some of which are quite elaborate. Music plays in the background and frequently new clothes are worn. Most importantly, however, the intercourse of congenial spirits abound.

Universities seem to understand that tailgaters are reliable, successful alumni whose consumption of drinks in the parking lot isn't a real threat. The usual college tailgate crowd consists of mostly college graduates, in a familiar setting, not apt to go wild because someone offers them a free drink. People in the tailgate areas police their own crowd. They know the personality of their parking lot and can spot interlopers and possible trouble. If people become offensive or dangerous in a particular group, security will be told and the problem

will be eliminated without pain. Each group, because of tough laws and the group's level of education, usually has a designated driver.

The survey on the following page shows which schools allow drinking and which prohibit it for their tailgaters. The survey was taken from the Athletic Departments at all Division One and Ivy League schools. Colleges are bound by the laws of their community and State. Sometimes they have no other choice than to enforce the law. In most cases, however, drinking alcoholic beverages in moderation is tolerated by schools.

Tale of Two Cities

O ne Saturday I traveled to two major college football games. In the morning I visited Iowa State (at Ames, 30 minutes north of Des Moines) who was to play against Oklahoma at noon. In spite of the apprehension these fans had about their Cyclones playing the Sooners, the Iowa State fans were congenial and enjoying their pregame tailgating. Nice-looking people in wool sweaters and plaids were unloading their upscale vehicles for the day. Grills,

Legal Drinking

Here is a list, compiled from our own survey, of colleges and universities that have no laws against the consumption of alcohol in their tailgating areas:

School	Location	Conference
Army	West Point, New York	Independent
Central Michigan	Mount Pleasant	MAC
Cincinnati	Cincinnati, Ohio	Independent
Colombia	New York, New York	Ivy League
Colorado	Boulder	Big Eight
Colorado State	Fort Collins	WAC
East Carolina	Greenville, North Carolina	Independent
Florida State	Tallahassee	ACC
Georgia	Athens	SEC
Georgia Tech	Atlanta	ACC
Indiana	Bloomington	Big Ten
Kent State	Kent, Ohio	MAC
Louisiana Tech	Ruston	Big West
Marshall	Huntington, West Virginia	Southern
Northern Illinois	DeKalb	Big West
Northwestern	Evanston, Illinois	Big Ten
Oregon State	Corvallas	PAC 10
Pennsylvania	Philadelphia	Ivy League
Rice	Houston, Texas	WAC
Rutgers	New Brunswick, New Jersey	Big East
San Diego State	San Diego	WAC
Stanford	Stanford, California	PAC 10
Texas	Austin	Big Eight
UNLV	Las Vegas	Big West
Wisconsin	Madison	Big Ten
Wyoming	Laramie	WAC
Yale	New Haven, Connecticut	Ivy League

Conference Standings:

WAC — 4	Big West — 3	PAC 10 — 2
Ivy League — 3	ACC — 2	Big East — 1
Big Ten — 3	Big Eight — 2	SEC — 1
Independent — 3	MAC — 2	Southern — 1

woks, picnic tables, director's chairs, and coolers could be seen while occasionally a football was tossed in the air. Red flags snapped in the breeze high above some vehicles. All around were the sounds of marching band music from CD and tape players. (With one exception, a "30-something group" was playing a Chubby Checker song and doing the twist.) It was one big party.

The game began and the Cyclones held the Sooners. In fact, Iowa State started off like they were going to pull the upset of the season. Leaving in the middle of the first quarter, I got away before the Sooners did pull ahead. My drive was 200 miles that day, but I took with me great memories of wonderful Iowa State fans enjoying their tailgate parties.

Minnesota was to play Indiana that night at the Metrodome, downtown Minneapolis's teflon roofed excuse for a stadium. After my

200 mile trek, I checked into a hotel, freshened up, and then headed for the Dome. I was excited to be attending yet another college football game in the same day. However, as soon as I pulled into the parking lot I began to feel as if I had stumbled onto a pro game instead.

I made two complete trips around the stadium looking for tailgaters, flags, or even fans. There were none. Only people, unsmiling, getting out of their cars, putting their heads down and heading briskly for the stadium. Finally, I saw a lady get out of a car, just west of the Dome, and head for her trunk. She was obviously fixing drinks, but when she saw me, she retreated back into the car where she and her husband were consuming sandwiches. I asked, through the window, if I could talk with them. They ignored me. Really! (They probably thought I was KGB.) Finally I showed them my survey and camera

The Metrodome parking lot before a Minnesota game: notice the number of tailgaters not out in the parking lot

and said that I was writing a book about tailgating. The lady cracked the window about an inch and said with pride, "We don't tailgate here, it's not legal." Also I later discovered that drinking is illegal in the downtown parking lots too. Good idea! Move the game away from campus and outlaw fun!

The game of football can be as fun and exciting as it is on college campuses or it can be dull like in an NFL Dome. Colleges that sell their souls to a city for a new stadium get what they deserve; a nice facility where there is no tradition, no fun, and eventually no fans.

By the way, the Dome game turned out in favor of the visiting Hoosiers, but nobody cared!

The Beer of Choice

Some people drink beer like "Inside the Beltway Yuppies." They buy a brand because it makes a statement. Just like a BMW in the driveway, they reason, Heinekens or Becks at the bar shows class. If there are no stylish beers available they probably drink bottled water.

Tailgaters, however, buy beer for thirst. There are two thirsts common

to college football fans. The first comes from hearty grilled sandwiches like Bratwurst with sauerkraut and onions slathered with brown mustard. The second comes from being outside, in the elements, yelling for the team. As long as the beer is cold and wet, it doesn't really matter. Tailgaters will generally drink any reasonable brand of beer, as long as it's cold.

If this sensible approach to hops is acceptable, then why are so many tailgaters hoisting better or more expensive brands? You may have to consult the "Commandments of Tailgating" to understand. The Eighth Commandment states that on labeled beverages that contain alcohol, it is acceptable to buy the more expensive brand for your guests. After all, a tailgate happens only a few times a year. You wouldn't order a cheap beer at the country club or in a fine restaurant, would you? Then why serve it to your real friends at a tailgate? Spend a little more money and get something special.

The real trick for the beer supplier at a tailgate is to serve something very good, yet unpretentious. Imports like Heineken, Corona, and Becks are available everywhere in America. They are acceptable at any tailgate, but they are served by people without imagination or taste as often as by people who like them. Wouldn't it be great to serve a beer, tasting just as good, but costing less? A beer that is much less common? A beer that's not available to everyone in the parking lot? To do this the tailgater has to search for the unusual.

A good way to find great tasting, less common beers is to look at regional brands. Rolling Rock beer has always been brewed in Latrobe, Pennsylvania. This once sleepy little brand was one of the original "Brewed from Mountain Spring Water" beers. It came in little 7 oz. green bottles with white painted labels. Canadian giant Labatts purchased Rolling Rock and made it available to the majority of US beer drinkers. The green bottle will still turn heads at a tailgate, but for how long?

Our goal, to find an official beer for *The Tailgater's Handbook*, prompted us to contact people all over the United States. We wrote letters, phoned and talked face-to-face with beer makers, beer drinkers and retailers all over the country. We found one of America's great beers in Wisconsin.

Leinenkugels', the official beer of *The Tailgater's Handbook*, gave us the best of all worlds. It made a statement. It tasted good. And it was not expensive like an import. Leinenkugels' was a once small brand known only in Wisconsin for great taste. It was born in Chippewa Falls in 1867 and marketed only a couple of hundred miles from it's home. Recently they began working with Miller Brewing and have started to spread to larger markets. Leinenkugels' is now one of the more popular "upscale" beers in Chicago and has made it all the way down to Southern Indiana. It's the perfect tailgate beer for many reasons, but most of all because people love it!

Leinenkugels' gives tours and has a gift shop and historic buildings at their Wisconsin home

Don't Drink and Drive

Staying sober, for tailgaters that drive, is a must. There are few things less enjoyable for guests than to be forced to ride with a driver with whom they've lost confidence. Every new situation becomes an adventure. Blood pressure tends to soar and silent prayers are common.

Most states are too lenient regarding their drunk driving laws. The words Blood Alcohol Concentration, abbreviated to BAC, represent the percentage of alcohol in the blood. The BAC gives our state governments a measuring stick by which they can make and enforce traffic laws to protect us from the actions of drunk drivers. A few states, California being the most populated, have a maximum legal BAC of .08. Most states, however, allow a .10 BAC. We refer to these laws as lenient because most of us are not sober at .10 BAC, or for that matter, we're not too "sharp" at .08 as well.

For years Mothers Against Drunk Driving (MADD), a 3 million member national organization, has lobbied for reduced BAC levels in judging whether a person is too drunk to drive. MADD would like to have all states set .08 as their level where drivers are judged to be drunk. The American Medical Association would like the BAC standard lowered to .05 and the Department of Health and

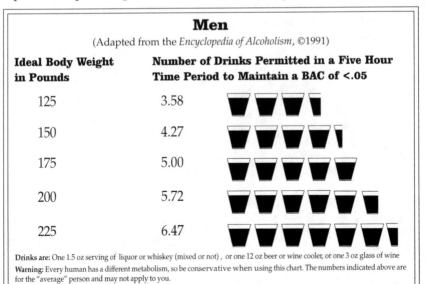

Men
(Adapted from the *Encyclopedia of Alcoholism*, ©1991)

Ideal Body Weight in Pounds	Number of Drinks Permitted in a Five Hour Time Period to Maintain a BAC of <.05	
125	3.58	
150	4.27	
175	5.00	
200	5.72	
225	6.47	

Drinks are: One 1.5 oz serving of liquor or whiskey (mixed or not), or one 12 oz beer or wine cooler, or one 3 oz glass of wine

Warning: Every human has a different metabolism, so be conservative when using this chart. The numbers indicated above are for the "average" person and may not apply to you.

Women

(Adapted from the *Encyclopedia of Alcoholism*, ©1991)

Ideal Body Weight in Pounds	Number of Drinks Permitted in a Five Hour Time Period to Maintain a BAC of <.05	
100	2.07	▼▼▌
125	2.59	▼▼▐
150	3.11	▼▼▼▌
175	3.6	▼▼▼▌

Drinks are: One 1.5 oz serving of liquor or whiskey (mixed or not) , or one 12 oz beer or wine cooler, or one 3 oz glass of wine
Warning: Every human has a different metabolism, so be conservative when using this chart. The numbers indicated above are for the "average" person and may not apply to you.

Human Services would like it lowered to .04 by the year 2000. [1]

If a situation arises that forces a person who has consumed alcohol to drive, read the accompanying charts to estimate if your BAC is below the legal driving level. This section has charts for both men and women to help determine their BAC after a five hour time period. Five hours allows for an hour and a half of tailgating and three and one half hours of football. The average for a man is a .015 BAC reduction per hour[2] and for women it is a .011 BAC reduction.[3] If a person must drive earlier than five hours after imbibing, these charts are not applicable.

Footnotes

1. *Health Magazine*, July/August 1994 page 64
2. *The Encyclopedia of Alcoholism* 2nd Edition, ©1991 page 49
3. *Mademoiselle Magazine*, January 1995, page 70

Tailgate Heat

In most areas of the country there are times when you'll find it almost too cold to tailgate. This is very discouraging to the chef who planned, purchased, and, in some cases, prepared all the food for the game. It is also inconvenient for the people who planned to eat at the party and are now faced with prospect of a hot dog from a vendor. Vendors don't sell cocktails, and they don't sell tasty desserts either. On very cold days, they are also out of hot chocolate and coffee when you finally get through the line to the counter to order.

Cold is a relative term which means something different to each person. One cannot simply rely on the thermometer to see if it's too cold to tailgate. There are other factors like wind, sunshine and precipitation that all can figure in the determination of how cold it is.

Wind chill, a formula which tells us how cold it feels, is a good measure for tailgaters to pay attention to. However, most tailgaters are smart enough to move out of the wind. If their parking lot is forgiving enough to allow them to park across the path of the wind or to picnic on the side of the vehicle that shelters them from the wind then there is no wind and the wind chill isn't a factor. If their lot is one of those reserved, numbered space, big-giver lots, they may have to take other measures. They may

need to erect a screen from the wind using an inexpensive tarp. If tailgaters can use two adjacent vehicles, making a screen with the tarp and a few bungee cords is simple.

Once the wind is eliminated as a factor, tailgaters need to work on a source of heat. If the day is sunny, there may be little need for extra heat. The sun beating down on the asphalt, dark clothing, vehicles and skin tends to make even a cold day feel good.

If there is no sun, it's time to use external sources. Things like proper clothing, hot foods and fires will help. The most common heating source for tailgaters is the barbecue grill. This cooking source will throw off plenty of heat while it cooks or warms your meal. Both the hot food and the flames will heat your body and warm your spirit.

Good ways to keep warm: the outdoor fireplace (above) and the bulk heater (right)

A fire is a good source of warmth and is, in some ways, similar to Kevin Costner's field in *Field of Dreams*. Build it and they will come. People seem to want to congregate around a fire. Maybe it's the memories of their youth — standing around the warming fire at the skating pond, sledding hill or scout camp-outs. The only problem with building a fire is the parking surface. If you are on dirt or gravel, the security guards will probably look the other way or join you for a toddy and a toasted marshmallow. But if you are on asphalt, you need to make other arrangements. There are a couple of great products out there from Weber and Coleman which will work even on paved lots. One is the Weber Outdoor Fireplace. They look like a big Weber grill with stronger legs and larger features. These large kettles hold a roaring fire safely above the pavement. They also operate with the Weber tradition of allowing the user to extinguish the heat simply by putting the lid down and suffocating the fire. Coleman's 15,000 BTU Bulk Heater will really throw off heat and is more of a gas space heater. Both these items are available at discount and camping outlets.

To build a fire at a game you need to either raid your fireplace wood supply or pick up a small bundle at a gas station convenience store. Be sure to have fire starters or some newspaper along too. If you bring your wood in a cardboard box, that box will make a good starter as well. You can tear off bits and pieces until both the box and the wood are gone.

Ten Coldest Tailgates*

Location	Average November Temperature
1. University of Minnesota**	33°
2. (3-way tie) University of Wyoming	35°
University of Maine	35°
Washington State University	35°
5. Dartmouth College	36°
6 (3-way tie) University of Colorado	37°
University of Wisconsin	37°
Penn State University	37°
9. (2-way tie) University of Nebraska	38°
Michigan State University	38°

* Big time schools in the lower 49 states
**There are still some truly dedicated fans in Minnesota who tailgate

The Recipe Not Received

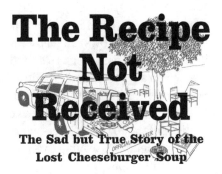

The Sad but True Story of the Lost Cheeseburger Soup

L ate in the '93 football season I road-tripped to Penn State to see tailgaters at a Nittany Lions' game against Indiana at Beaver Stadium. I left Indy Friday morning bound for my first destination, a friend's ski condo in the mountains southeast of Pittsburgh. This was to be a reunion of sorts because the condo was owned by a close friend, a Penn State alumnus and great host, who I hadn't visited in quite some time.

The drive was typical for late fall. The air was cold and most of the leaves had turned to a deep brown. I set my cruise control at 69 mph and went into my "auto pilot mode." That's where I relax and forget about vehicles passing mine. The flatlands around Indy, in an hour or so, changed to rolling hills just before the Ohio line, and as I approached Pennsylvania the hills became larger. The interstate (I-70) became a series of huge gradual ramps which rose between hills, taking the least expensive route while trying to maintain a general direction. Here, large trucks had a hard time maintaining their speeds while climbing and a harder time containing them while descending. The drive became a game of avoiding the trucks on the right while going up a hill and staying out of the way of the trucks on the left while going down.

Just about dark I entered the mountains in Pennsylvania. The unusual thing about these mountains is that they abruptly appear with a very definite steep ridge, just like the edge of a table with a long cloth to the floor. As I drove up this ridge my vehicle ascended about 2000 feet in just a few miles. My ears popped several times. Also the higher I drove, the colder it became. There was now snow on the ground. I sensed that I was approaching ski country.

Now off the turnpike, there was a different type of traffic. Instead of truck drivers with cigarettes and CBs there were couples with bottled water and car phones. People from the city passed me en route to the mountains with skis atop their cars. They were off for adventure, just like me.

My evening with Dick and Linda Truxel, condo owners and Penn State grads, was perfect. Linda had prepared chicken and Dick created one of his famous Caesar salads. After dinner we consumed adult beverages by the fireplace. Plans were devised and revised for

Saturday, game day! We eventually settled on a joint breakfast, early, then I would depart ahead of them for State College. I needed to be at the stadium early enough to catch plenty of tailgaters. They planned to arrive only about an hour or so before the game. With my camera loaded, my survey forms readied, clothes laid out and the car packed for a quick departure, all I needed was a good night's sleep.

Saturday dawned with clouds and fresh snow on the slopes. With trepidation and anticipation, I headed eastward. When people give directions to Penn State the first words out of their mouths are, "you can't get there from here". (That's because there are no direct roads do to the parallel mountain ridges). The best route to the game was southeast on the Turnpike and then north through Altoona. The problems with these roads are that they are crowded and narrow. Probably an hour of the drive is on two lane roads or right though small towns. The advantage is the scenery. Up from Altoona the road widens and goes northeast along the eastern slope of a beautiful valley. That's when the sun decided to come out and I thought that this may be the prettiest drive to campus I've seen. The sun highlighted the valley and the mountains on the other side, maybe five or ten miles west. It was breath taking.

Close to State College the highway widens into a freeway. Then you see the altar of college football (Beaver Stadium) towering above its pews (grass meadows) all ready for its tailgating parishioners. I selected a space on a farm of the Agriculture School. One thing I observed about Nittany Lion fans is that they arrive early. Before 10:00 am there were parking attendants waving cars into rapidly filling lots.

Parking is predominantly grass with some paved lots very close to the stadium. The fans consequently have the advantage of a soft surface under foot and a good place to build a fire, put up a canopy/tent and set up a flag. The whole Penn State panorama has the appearance of being a Civil War battlefield. The trails of smoke from fires and grills look like the cook fires of soldiers of 130 years ago. The variety of flags flying from vehicles appear to be some sort of regimental colors. The tents made from tarps surrounded by blue clad fans had a strange resemblance to a Union encampment, not too far to the southeast in Gettysburg.

Penn State fans do something that people don't do at other stadiums. They fly flags other than the standard school type. Instead of just a Nittany Lion or a PSU on a blue background, the Lion fans fly ethnic and state flags. A person of proud Swedish heritage will fly a flag of Sweden. Someone with Polish parents will fly the red and white colors. There are flags from all over the world! Then there are flags to prove how far from the stadium you live. People had Maryland, Ohio, New, Jersey, Florida, Texas and even California state flags.

My approach to strangers is to announce that I am writing a book about tailgating and to ask for the head tailgater (there is generally one person that everyone points out). Then I get the people to complete a survey, share a recipe, and then pose for a few snap shots. Often I sample foods, and occasionally I take a drink of something, depending on the availability of Port-o-lets.

A parking space somewhere behind Dicks and Linda's was occupied by a party of Penn State tailgaters that even had some Hoosiers in it from Fort Wayne. We struck up a conversation and everyone posed for a group shot. The woman in charge of the food at this party was a "pro". She offered me samples of foods that were delicious. I tasted and tasted while passing time waiting for the Truxels.

All of a sudden this party of tailgaters, on command, lined up with plastic bowls. Somebody handed me one and then we proceeded past a huge pot of soup. Each of us were given a bowl of this mixture. I tried the soup and couldn't believe my taste buds. This had to be the best soup I ever tasted. The best soup ever made ..in the world! This soup tasted like a grilled cheeseburger. Not one from McDonalds, but one from a country club that's large and juicy with onion and pickles. Just like a cheeseburger you'd barbecue on your back yard grill. It was delicious. And the chef, bless her heart, dolled out a round of seconds too. Everyone got in line for seconds, except me. I went over to where the Truxels parked and brought them back to this soup. We got bowls and went up to the pot and there was nothing. It was finished. All that was left was a residue of cheese in the bottom of the pot. If there had been no one around I'd have gotten a bun and dipped it out.

There were recipe forms in my tailgating folder. I retrieved a form and got the chef to agree to send me the recipe for this "super soup". I felt better knowing that my family and I would be satisfied all winter long consuming great quantities of the world's greatest soup. There was a picture in my mind of my children's faces as Dad served up this delicious soup. Life was good and going to get even better. I could relax and even go into the stadium for the football game.

To no one's surprise Indiana lost, but the game was not decided until very late in the fourth quarter. The weather was great as was the half time show. The scenery was even greater from inside the stadium. All was right with the world.

After returning to Indiana, my standard conversation always returned to that soup. I promised everyone that I would be making the best soup they have ever eaten. All I had to do was wait for the recipe to arrive at my post office box.

I waited and waited. In fact I'm still waiting. The recipe hasn't come yet. Usually recipes will arrive a week or two after I request them from fans at a game. It's been over two years and this recipe isn't here yet. I don't think it's coming.

My family has tried to console me. They say I'll find better recipes. They say I'll forget about it. But every time I see the word Cheeseburger in print, on TV or hear it spoken my mind pictures the empty pot and my empty post office box. I know I'll never find another soup as good. I know that just printing that recipe would have made me thousands of friends for life. But, as of today, 692 days since that game, there is no Cheeseburger Soup recipe in my box; I know, I just checked.

Protect Your Food
(and the Party)

Watch the crowd around you at a football game. Is there someone who looks like they are a little worse for wear? Do they make too frequent trips to the toilet? Then be sure you don't eat what they ate. They probably found some new friends (in their food) before the game.

These new friends are the opportunistic bugs (bacteria) with fancy names that team up with unsafe food handling to lay us low with the

---

The Nine Meanest Bumper Stickers

The following bumper stickers were noted during travels for The Tailgater's Handbook. *They are ranked in order of their degree of hostility or lack of taste. Number 9 is the mildest and 1 is the meanest.*

9. Purdue is The Indiana University
8. Tar Heel by birth, Blue Devil by choice
7. My two favorite teams are UCLA and whoever is playing USC
6. Friends don't let friends go to Texas
5. The dumbest student at MIT transferred to Harvard. Raised the average IQ of both schools
4. Ohio is a four letter word
3. Keep America beautiful, run over an Aggie
2. Muck Fishigan
1. Root for Rutgers or Vito will kill you.

...urants. Three children died and ...dreds of people became sick from ...bacteria. The problem of getting rid ...E.Coli" was solved by raising the ...king temperature of beef patties ...n about 140 degrees to 155 degrees ...to add 30 seconds more to their ...king time. The epidemic stopped. ...FDA recommends that restaurants ...e the temperature for beef cooking ...55 degrees simply because bacteria ...killed by this much heat .

If you are looking for some ...pful, healthy rule of thumb here is ...best one. **Always keep hot foods and cold foods cold**. This means ...foods kept above 140 degrees and ...d foods kept below 40 degrees will ...allow the growth of bacteria. And ...king hot foods at a high enough

temperature (above 145 degrees) will actually kill the bacteria.

Most refrigerator temperatures are set for 40 degrees or below. Some groups like the Purdue University COOP Extension Service recommend 37 degrees. At these low temperatures bacteria are present, but they are dormant. If we start with foods that are as low as possible in bacteria and store them properly, we can eat them or cook them and not get sick.

Keeping hot foods hot and cold foods cold at the tailgate is just as important and just as easy as in the kitchen. There are portable stoves and grills to cook and keep hot foods hot. There are insulated coolers which keep cold foods cold. All you have to do is follow our clean rules.

Rules of the Chef

The following "Rules of the Chef" have ...een adapted from a list of rules found ...n the bulletin board of the Chef's Office ...n the cruise ship Queen Elizabeth II.

1. The Chef is right.

2. The Chef is always right.

3. The Chef does not eat, he nourishes himself.

4. The Chef does not drink, he tastes.

5. The Chef is not late, he is delayed.

6. If you criticize the Chef, you criticize the Almighty.

7. All Chef's decisions are final unless he changes his mind.

above mentioned nasty symptoms. There are three basic types of bacteria that are most common in food poisoning. They are *Salmonella*, *Staphlococcus* and *Clostridium Perfringens*. Salmonella, the single biggest cause of food poisoning and one of the more infamous bugs, affects some 2.5 million people every year. Most food born illnesses, however,

won't kill you. The sy[mptoms] cause usually last on[ly] except with the very ol[d] or people who's immu[ne] affected by another illn[ess]

In 1993, however, [the] infamous outbreak of f[ood poisoning] caused by *Escherichia* [coli, a] dangerous type bug [at a] Pacific Northwest Ja[ck]

res[...] hu[...] thi[...] of [...] co[...] fro[...] an[...] co[...] Th[...] ra[...] to [...] are[...]

he[...] th[...] **ho**[...] ho[...] co[...] no[...] cc[...]

Clean Food Rules

1. **Start clean** with fresh foods for the lowest possible chance of contamination. Buy USDA meats and look at freshness dates on everything.

2. **Stay clean** by preparing foods properly to eliminate cross contamination. Wash hands, cutting board, utensils and the rest.

3. **Store clean:** When packing for the tailgate be sure to refrigerate all perishable foods the night before or at least long enough to get their temperature below 40 degrees. Then put them right into an insulated cooler like those from Igloo with enough ice to maintain the cold temperature. Use sealed containers to prevent foods from cross contamination or other sources of bacteria. Keep the cooler in the shade during travel and tailgating.

4. **Serve clean** by using snap sealed food storage containers like those by Rubbermaid to serve as well as transport the food. Use clean serving utensils and have enough so that you can have clean utensils

after the game for sec[ond] helpings. Seal every[thing] not serving. Put it bac[k] to get its temperature [below] 40 degrees pronto. Ma[ke sure] hot foods are cooked [enough to] kill any bacteria and th[ey are hot] enough (above 140 de[grees)].

5. **Store clean again.** Put [foods away] after eating. Cook on[ly so] that there are no lefto[ver] foods unless you plan [a] cooler for them alone a[nd] reheat them enough be[fore] eating. Put the foods [in] coolers out of the sun, i[n shade] when finished with the[m. Make] sure windows are ope[n to] keep the vehicle a little [cooler.]

6. **Stop clean.** After the pr[e or] game tailgating be sure [there are] no leftovers. Throw awa[y foods] that have been left out [and] gotten warm enough [to grow] bacteria. Don't take foo[d] for that night time snac[k unless] you have kept then[m in the] insulated cooler, as [cold as] possible, all day.

Maximum Food Storage Times

Freezer		Refrigerator	
Bars	6-9 months	Baked Beans	3 days
Baked Beans	2 weeks	Bratwurst	1 day
Bratwurst	1-3 months	Cheese	4-8 weeks
Cake	6 months	Cream Cheese	1-2 weeks
Chicken & Wings	3-4 months	Chicken & Wings	1-2 days
Chili	3 months	Chili	2-3 days
Cookies	12 months	Corn on the Cob	1-2 days
Corn on the Cob	8 months	Deviled Eggs	1-2 days
Fruits	9-12 months	Dips (with creams)	1-2 days
Hamburger	3-4 months	Fruits:	
Ham	3-4 months	Berry and Cherry	1-2 days
Hot Dogs	1 month	Hamburger	1-2 days
Lunch Meat	1-2 months	Ham	3-4 days
Pie	6 months	Hot Dogs	4-5 days
Pizza	6 months	Lunch Meat	3-5 days
Pork Sausage	1-2 months	Pie	2-3 days
Ribs	3-4 months	Pizza	2-3 days
Sandwiches	1 month	Pork Sausage	1 day
Shrimp	4 months	Potato Salad	1-2 days
Soups	3 months	Ribs	3-4 days
Steaks	6-12 months	Salads	1-2 days
		Sandwiches	1 day
		Shrimp	1-2 days
		Soup	3 days
		Steaks	2 days
		Veggies (for dip)	1-2 weeks

Regional Tastes from A to Z

Match tailgater's taste choices with the tailgating college closest to the best source of that food. For example, a tailgater's favorite drink is beer and beer is available from large and small breweries across Wisconsin. So the answer for the letter "F" is 26 — Wisconsin. Some states have more than one speciality, and some specialties have more than one state.

Why, you are asking, is this important? Because if you are planning to go to Wisconsin, don't bring your own beer. Buy it there! Experiment with local brands. Soak up some local color.

Key to Map:

1. Boston College	10. Memphis	19. Pittsburgh
2. California	11. Miami	20. Purdue
3. Cincinnati	12. Michigan State	21. South Dakota
4. Columbia	13. Minnesota	22. Syracuse
5. Dartmouth	14. Northwestern	23. UTEP
6. E. Carolina	15. Notre Dame	24. Washington
7. Georgia	16. Oklahoma State	25. W. Michigan
8. Kansas	17. Ole Miss	26. Wisconsin
9. Louisville	18. Penn State	

Write the number for the college closest to the source of each food. Some have more than one answer. Check your answers with the key below.

A. Apples _____

B. Barbecue Pork _____

C. Bars _____

D. Barbecue Sauce _____

E. Creamy Potato Salad _____

F. Beer _____

G. Baked Beans _____

H. Hot Potato Salad _____

I. Chips _____

J. Pretzels _____

K. Bourbon _____

L. Hot Dogs _____

M. Barbecue Ribs _____

N. Bratwurst _____

O. Cheese _____

P. Chocolate _____

Q. Hoagie Sandwiches _____

R. Chili _____

S. Hot Wings _____

T. Key Lime Pie _____

U. Olives _____

V. Pecan Pie _____

W. Pancakes with Syrup _____

X. Peanuts _____

Y. Pizza _____

Z. Popcorn _____

ZA. Wine _____

Key:

A 12, 24	F 26	K 9, 14	P 18	Z 15
B 6	G 1	L 4	Q 19	U 2
C 13	H 21	M 10	R 3, 22	V 17	ZA 2
D 8, 16	I 25	N 26	S 22	X 7
E 20	J 18	O 26	T 11	Y 14

What's for Lunch?

The main ingredients for a successful tailgate party are good food and creativity! I once heard a wife (Sue Ellen) ask her husband (Joe) what could be added to a dish to improve the taste. His answer, "kerosene." That's not exactly the way to encourage long pleasurable tailgating! Because people sometimes try things that others won't eat doesn't mean that their tailgates are doomed. They should just make sure that they have plenty of other foods that are time-tested winners so that everyone is satisfied and there is still room for creativity and experimentation. That is how Steak Tartar became hamburger.

During the last three years we surveyed people tailgating at many college games in different parts of the country. We wanted to determine what people liked to eat and drink. There were surveys for both warm and cold weather tailgating. These surveys included the main courses, side dishes, desserts and drinks.

This portion of the handbook is designed to help your menu planning with our survey results and recipes collected from fellow tailgaters, as well as recipes from renowned authors/chefs. Where these appear we have tried to picture the cover of their book or magazine so you can buy a copy for yourself.

Main Course Survey: Warm Weather

What is your favorite main course for warm weather tailgating? Almost 200 tailgaters were interviewed over a two year period at ten stadiums. There were 127 replies to this question.

Choice	Number	Percent
1. Bratwurst	40	31.0
2. Sandwiches	33	25.6
3. Hamburgers	17	13.2
4. Chicken	16	12.4
5. Hot Dogs	7	5.4
6. Ethnic	4	3.1
7. Salads	3	2.3
8. Ribs	3	2.3
9. Pork	2	1.5
10. Sausage	2	1.5

Brats & Sausages

OFFICIAL TAILGATER

According to *Gourmet* magazine the Chinese were making sausages in 1122 BC or before. Homer mentioned "grilled wursts" in the *Odyssey*. And early colonists observed Indians making smoked sausages. Richard Gehman, author of *The Sausage Book* says that sausage making really came into flower in the Middle Ages. Most were named for their town of origin (like Bologna for Bologna, Italy), but others, like the Dachshund, got their names in a more unusual manner. In 1852 members of the Frankfurt, Germany Sausage Guild invented a new sausage modeled after a Dachshund dog which belonged to one of the members. This Dachshund Sausage came to America, but quickly got a new name because a columnist in New York had a problem spelling Dachshund. He coined the name Hot Dog. The name caught on and the dog swept America.

Today's commercial pork sausage making probably stems from the daily operation of butcher shops. People constantly asked the butcher for lean cuts of pork. What was left were residual trimmings too fatty for sale; what a waste of good pork! Determined to find a use for the meat, the butcher began experimenting and found that by adding starch, salt and seasonings to the meat he was able to obtain a mix that had an acceptable flavor after cooking. After closing the mix in a natural skin and twisting it into portions, the sausage rope was invented!

Today's sausages, hot dogs, and bratwurst all stem from this early butcher determined to make a profit; however, competition, innovation and government regulation have greatly improved these products. Producers today use better cuts of meat, utilize better storage methods, process ingredients more efficiently, keep more juices in the meat, control the quality, and have even invented edible artificial casings.

Our survey of tailgaters shows that more people (38%) prefer sausages to other warm weather main courses. The second choice to sausages was sandwiches. The high appeal of sausages can be attributed to the fact that they are easy to eat, have character and bold taste. It's also pretty hard to ruin sausages during cooking. About the only thing a tailgater can do wrong to a sausage is to burn it. I think, however, another reason that sausages are so popular for Saturday's game are that American diets have changed. People now eat so many low fat foods regularly that they have a natural desire to let down on a few game days each fall. Of sausage preferences in warm weather, bratwurst was the choice of 81%, hot dogs 14% and other sausages 5%. (In cold weather many tailgaters understandably switch their preference to hot chili. However, 20% still pick brats.)

To talk to an expert about bratwurst we contacted David Finch (a born and raised Midwesterner -'88 Northwestern) who works at Johnsonville Foods, the industry's leader. Johnsonville Foods, named after the east central Wisconsin town where they started on a small scale, now markets brats nationally. Their most famous product, Original Brats are now complemented by many options. They sell Beer 'n Brat, Cheesy Beer 'n Brat, Irish O' Garlic, Beef Brats, and even Brat Patties. They have many other sausages including Polish and Italian. David's title, by the way, is "To Spread The Good Word About Johnsonville's Big Taste." Or, TSTGWAJBT for short! Obviously, Johnsonville doesn't believe in fancy titles, or even suits or neck ties.

Mr. Finch, TSTGWAJBT, suggests that brats be slightly precooked prior to grilling. They can be simmered for 20 minutes in beer, beer and onion, or water. He cautions, however, that the brats are never touched with sharp metal objects which could pierce the casing. Real brat gourmets desire the tasty sausage juices inside the wurst. For that reason, brat aficionados have developed creative ways to prevent piercing; for instance, some use a new

For big bratwurst fans, it might be worthwhile to look into the Johnsonville Big Taste Grill for your next big event. They cook more than 2500 brats at a time.

pair of canvas gloves soaked in water. As you turn the brats (wearing gloves instead of using utensils), you also drip water on the coals. This keeps the flare-ups to a minimum. Another idea David suggests is to have a mist water sprayer by the grill. Then you can mist the coals and prevent ashes from splashing up onto the brats. By the way, you don't grill brats, I was informed, you fry them. Even though you are using a grill, it is called a brat fry, at least it is in Sheboygan, where bratwurst is considered a health food.

All bratwurst, unless otherwise specified on their label, need to be cooked. Most American brats also contain pork, which generally requires a little more care in preparation. Be sure to look on the package of your bratwursts for instructions or use one of our safe recipes that follow to make sure you have perfectly tasty, but also safely cooked, brats.

Brats in Beer

Ingredients required:

2 lbs. uncooked bratwurst sausages
12 oz. bottle of beer
water

The Night Before:

Place brats into a large cooking pot. Pour beer over the brats then add water to mostly cover individual sausages. Bring the liquid to a boil and then reduce the heat. Simmer for 20 minutes, turning the brats carefully (with your fingers or a wooden spoon which will not puncture to casings). Make sure that the brats cook completely on both sides, losing their pink color.

Remove the brats from the pot and gently pat them dry with a paper towel. Refrigerate these sausages in a Rubbermaid Servin' Saver square storage container.

Game Day:

Grill the brats over medium heat. Be careful to brown all sides and not puncture the casings. Serve on harder rolls or buns with brown mustard and other toppings like onions or dill pickles.

To make Brats in Water, simply substitute water for the beer called for above. You might also want to add a whole, medium-sized, peeled onion to the water for additional flavor.

The Hamburger

Contrary to popular belief, the hamburger didn't come from Germany. The medieval Tartars (on what is now the steps of Russia) were the first to eat ground meat. It seems they would put ground meat under their saddle for the whole day's ride. Then they scraped it up, added onion juice, salt and pepper and ate it raw. Thus the roots of Steak Tartar!

Merchants from Hamburg, Germany brought this dish back "From Russia With Love" to Germany and named it the Hamburg Steak. Later they began to broil it.

There is a dispute about who served the first American hamburger. The first burger was served at either the 1904 St Louis World's Fair or Louis (Lassur's) Lunch in New Haven, Connecticut the same year. In 1967 Lassur's place was designated a landmark in New Haven as the sight of the first American hamburger. History doesn't tell us, but Louie must have been a Yale fan!

We've included a couple of unusual hamburger recipes. Good

hamburgers start the night before as patties. Form them with your hands on a clean cutting board. These patties should be round and only slightly wider than the spatula which will be used to turn them. Make each about an inch thick to prevent them from cooking too fast. As you form patties place them on waxed paper four to a layer. These layers should be packed in a sealable container and refrigerated until they are packed in to the food cooler on game day.

For best grilling results, cook the burgers on a grill or basket (also called a rack) coated with vegetable oil spray about four to six inches above the coals. Cook the bottom side for about five minutes or until it is browned to your liking. Then turn the burger over and cook the other side five minutes for rare, seven for medium and ten for well done. Use a knife to cut into a burger to check its stage of readiness.

Most grill baskets will cook four to six burgers at a time, but allow the chef little flexibility to move individual meats to vary cooking speeds.

Use firmer buns like Kaiser rolls or onion buns, and don't skimp on the toppings. Condiments should include thick slices from big sweet (Vidalia) onions, fresh large slices of tomato, lengthwise sliced crispy dill pickles, fresh lettuce and several varieties of spicy mustards. Go ahead and add mayo or catsup if you must!

The Healthy Burger

Ruth Winter, author of *The Consumer Guide to Medicines in Food: Nutraceuticals that Help Prevent and Treat Physical and Emotional Illness*, concocted this healthy burger at the request of *Financial World Magazine*. It appeared in their September 12, 1995 issue.

Ingredients required (for each burger):

¼ lb. 85-90% fat free chopped beef
1 tbsp. oatmeal
2 tbsp. flaxseed or olive oil
1 clove garlic, minced
¼ tsp. reduced sodium soy sauce
a drop of red pepper

To Prepare:

Mix all above ingrediants together and form a patty. Broil the burger to your liking.

What Makes the Healthy Burger So Healthy?

We thought you'd never ask. Let's look at the reasoning:

- *Beef* contains vitamin B12 for a healthy nervous system and normal red blood cell formation. Beef also contains proteins from which neurotransmitters are derived.
- *Oatmeal* reduces cholesterol.
- *Flaxseed* or *Olive Oil* contains omega 3 fatty acids, which are good for the heart.
- *Garlic* lowers cholesterol and is an anticancer and anti-infection ingredient.
- *Red Pepper* is good for arthritis or lung problems.

Financial World *is not known for creating tantalizing treats, but with the advent of the healthy hamburger, all that might change.*

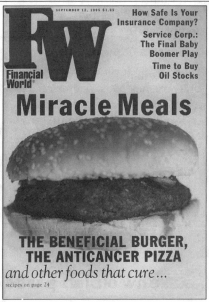

SEPTEMBER 12, 1995 $1.95

How Safe Is Your Insurance Company?

Service Corp.: The Final Baby Boomer Play

Time to Buy Oil Stocks

Financial World®

Miracle Meals

THE BENEFICIAL BURGER, THE ANTICANCER PIZZA
and other foods that cure...

recipes on page 24

Award-Winning Turkey Burgers

Ann Jones, a '92 Purdue graduate, won Purdue's National Tailgating Contest with these "heart-healthy" burgers. This recipe appears courtesy of the *Purdue Alumnus* magazine.

Ingredients required:

2½ lbs. lean ground turkey breast
2 egg whites
¼ cup seasoned bread crumbs
2 tbsp. Heinz 57 sauce
2 tbsp. A-1 sauce
½ tsp. Worchestershire sauce
¼ tsp. garlic powder
salt and pepper to taste

The Night Before:

Mix all ingredients in a large bowl. Form patties to your desired size and place them on waxed paper. Store the patties overnight in a serve and seal container in the refrigerator.

On Game Day:

Make a foil surface on your grill so the more fragile turkey burgers don't fall through the wires. Use cooking spray on the foil to prevent sticking. Grill the burgers until the juices run clean and the meat is completely cooked.

Tailgaters Tip:

When using turkey, don't skimp on garnishes. Most people relate a grilled burger as much to the onions, pickles and mustard taste as they do to a charbroiled beef taste.

The Sandwich

John Montagu (1718-1792), English nobleman, served a full life for his government. He sat in the House of Lords, held numerous government positions, ran the British Navy during the American Revolutionary War, and even had an American state named for him. Montagu, however, was more famous and useful to tailgaters because of his love for gambling.

In 1762 he was busy at a gaming table for 24 hours straight. Desiring food, but not wanting to leave the table, he ordered a servant to place cold beef between two slices of bread. He was able to continue his gambling and eat. Thus the birth of the modern sandwich! The name comes from the fact that Montagu, besides becoming First Lord of the English Admiralty,

The crest of the Earl of Sandwich

was born the Fourth Earl of Sandwich. In 1778, Captain James Cook was so thankful for Montagu's invention that he named a group of islands in the Pacific after him, The Sandwich Islands (known today as Hawaii).

After Montagu's first roast beef sandwich, his title lent its name to a wave which swamped the world. The word sandwich has been incorporated into many languages. The sandwich became important in Western and many Eastern cuisines because it was simple, portable and offered great variety. The English consume tea sandwiches. The Scandinavian *smorrebrod* are served open faced with toppings. The French even hollow out loaves and stuff them for sandwiches.

Sandwiches, however, probably were around earlier than the 18th century. Archaeologists have discovered that Swiss lake dwellers made bread out of flour and water over 8000 years ago. In about 3000 BC the Egyptians discovered that bread would raise with yeast. Surely some of these early tailgaters put some sort of filling between pieces of their bread.

Assuming that all "real" tailgaters know how to make their favorite sandwich, this section will deal only with a couple of varieties which work great at tailgate parties. Just as the Earl was an innovator, tailgaters need to experiment to find new ideas that work better, especially with sandwiches.

Brunswick Roll

Rosemary Bass serves this bread topper at Wisconsin games. She says she got the recipe 25 years ago from "who knows where." It tastes great on dark bread with a cold beer.

Ingredients Required:

1 2 lb. roll braunschweiger, very cold
1 8 oz. package cream cheese, softened
1 can of Oscar Mayer real bacon bits

To Prepare:

Peel off the casing on the braunshweiger. Using the cream cheese as icing, completely cover the outside of the braunshweiger. Roll the meat in bacon bits until it is evenly coated. Slice and serve on pumpernickel bread.

Illini Totem Rolls
(as in Totem Poles, get it?)

LaVonne Smith, a loyal Brave in the Illini tribe, makes these totem rolls for cold weather Illinois games.

Ingredients Required:

1 lb. ground beef
1 envelope onion soup mix
$^3/_4$ tsp. oregano
$^1/_8$ tsp. garlic salt
$^1/_2$ cup catsup

2 8 oz. packages of crescent rolls
   (LaVonne prefers the cheese variety)
1 cup shredded mozzarella cheese
poppy seeds for garnish (optional)

To Prepare:

Brown the beef and then drain off all the fat. Stir in the soup mix, oregano, garlic salt and catsup. Let mixture cool slightly. Separate each package of rolls into four rectangular sections consisting of two triangles separated by a perforation. Cut each section in half, making two long rectangles. Place rolls on an ungreased cookie sheet and press the perforations together. Place the meat mixture along the center of the dough rectangle and sprinkle with cheese. Bring sides of dough together overlapping the center and covering the meat and cheese. Seal this seam and both ends. Sprinkle with poppy seeds. Bake at 375 degrees or until golden brown. Cool slightly and then place the totem rolls in foil for transportation to the football game.

(University of) Kentucky Fried Chicken

While visiting a Kentucky Wildcat game, I tasted some great fried chicken. The cook, wishing to remain anonymous, contributed this recipe for everyone to enjoy. She said that this is the REAL Kentucky fried chicken.

Ingredients Required:

1½ cups vegetable oil   ½ tsp. paprika
1½ cups self rising flour   1 egg
1 tsp. salt   water
½ tsp. pepper   2½ to 3 lb. fryer chicken cut into pieces

The Night Before:

Heat oil in a skillet (iron skillet works best) to medium level. Mix flour, salt, pepper and paprika in plastic bag. Combine egg and two or three tablespoons of water and beat slightly in a separate bowl. Dip chicken in egg mixture than place into flour bag. Coat each piece of chicken (one at a time) in the bag. Fry the chicken 20 minutes on each side. Drain the chicken on a paper towel. Wrap in tinfoil and refrigerate.

Game Day:

You can either serve the chicken cold, with pasta salad, cole slaw or baked beans, or you can reheat it by placing it on the grill in its foil wrappings.

Main Course Survey: Cold Weather

What is your favorite main course for cold weather tailgating? Almost 200 tailgaters were interviewed over a two year period at ten stadiums. There were 136 replies to this question.

Choice	Number	Percent
1. Chili	64	45
2. Bratwurst	26	18
3. Chicken	16	11
4. Soup	11	8
5. Hamburgers	9	6
6. Ribs	5	4
7. Sandwiches	3	2
8. Sausage	2	1

Mike Bedosky's Hot Chicken Sandwich

Mike Bedosky provided Missouri tailgaters with great entertainment. He was, as a matter of fact, dubbed Mizzou's Mr. Everything. He joined the NFL Falcons and later the Browns. His recipe comes from *All-Pro Recipes*, a collection of recipes by NFL players published by Masters Press.

Ingredients Required:

1 loaf white bread
1 large box Velveeta cheese
4 cups of milk
8 chicken breasts
6 eggs
dash of salt and pepper

The Night Before:

Line the bottom of a 9 x 13" baking dish with slices of the white bread, crusts removed. Grill the chicken breasts and cut them into one inch cubes. Cover the bread with the chicken. Slice Velveeta into thin slices and cover the chicken with a layer of the cheese slices. Top all with another layer of the bread slices. In a separate bowl, mix eggs, milk, salt and pepper. Pour the mixture over the top layer of bread, cover with foil and refrigerate overnight.

Game Day:

Bake dish at 350 degrees for one hour or until bread is golden brown. Allow dish at least 30 minutes to cool before cutting into 12 squares. Serves 6.

You Need This Book!

Recommended reading for all tailgate chefs, *All-Pro Recipes* is a handy reference for everybody who likes to eat, watch football or both. It sells for $14.95 and is published by Masters Press of Indianapolis.

Irish Chili

When touring the Notre Dame parking lot on a snowy day you build up a powerful hunger for chili. Jan Putz serves the best chili in the whole lot. She likes to bring it to Irish games when the weather gets below 50 degrees. Even the parking lot employees make their way over to Jan's chili line.

Ingredients required:

2 lbs. 98% fat-free beef
½ cup finely diced green pepper
1 cup finely diced onion
1 tsp. Lawrey's Seasoned Salt
pepper and garlic to taste
1 qt. canned tomatoes

1 10 oz. can tomato soup plus can of water
2 16 oz. cans dark red kidney beans with liquid
1 4 oz. pack Carroll Shelby Chili Mix

The Day Before (at least):

Brown beef with peppers and onion. Add Lawrey's salt, pepper and garlic. Drain off the fat. Add tomatoes, soup, water, beans and chili mix. Simmer for one hour. Refrigerate.

Game Day:

Reheat in pot on grill or stove. Serve with oyster crackers and finely grated cheddar cheese.

The Putz Family: (from left to right) George, Bunnie, Jan and Todd

Turkey Chili

If you are ever at an Indiana game on a cold day, you are apt to see my wife, Cindy, serving her great-tasting chili. It has big hunks of tomatoes, which make you feel warm.

Ingredients Required:

2 lbs. ground turkey
3 pkgs. McCormick's Chili Mix
3 28 oz. cans whole peeled tomatoes, undrained
4 15 oz. cans dark red kidney beans, undrained
shredded cheddar cheese for topping

To Prepare:

Brown and drain turkey in large pot. Stir in seasoning, tomatoes and kidney beans. Bring to a boil and cover. Simmer, stirring occasionally, for one hour.

To Serve:

Serve topped with cheese along with hunks of French bread. Some people like to use "throw-away" bowls and plastic spoons, but you can find nice unbreakable serving vessels that add just a little more class to your party.

Warning:

Unless you tailgate with a bunch of wimps, your guests will consume more than one bowl of chili each.

Transportation and Storage:

This chili should always be made the night before the game and stored in a Rubbermaid Servin' Saver 1.1 gallon square container or a one gallon plastic ice cream bucket. There will be more than a gallon of chili from this recipe so save the rest for another day. Put your container into the refrigerator for the night and then into your food cooler for transportation. At the stadium, place your chili into a large cooking pot, cover it and heat it on your grill or Coleman stove. Heat the chili until it is hot. Be sure to allow enough time so you can heat this mixture slowly to prevent burning the bottom layers.

Tailgater's Onion Soup

This soup and I go back at least 20 years to my "French Gourmet Cooking Period." It was great at dinner parties for an early course. Later I discovered T.G.I. Friday's onion soup with the very thick layer of cheeses. This recipe is a combination of the good taste of real French Onion soup and the cheese of Friday's soup, adapted strictly for tailgating. This is great in cold weather.

Ingredients Required:

1 lb. onions sliced	4 tbsp. butter
2 tsp. fine sugar	salt (not with bullion)
2 heaping tbsp. flour	pepper
8 cups beef stock (or melt 10 bul-	french bread
lion cubes in 8 cups of hot water)	Gruyere or Mozzarella cheese

The Night Before:

In a soup pot, brown onions slowly in butter until they become transparent. Add sugar and cook three more minutes. Add flour and cook one minute. Add beef stock and bring the mixture to a boil while stirring. Simmer 20 minutes. Add salt and pepper to taste. Cool the soup, pour into a large canister and refrigerate.

Slice french bread, on an angle, so it almost fits the top of our soup bowls. Each piece should be about an inch thick. Place the slices on a large sheet of aluminum foil (dull side down) in a toaster oven or your broiler and toast one side. Remove the bread and turn it over. Put a gob of your favorite cheese on the untoasted side and return the bread to your oven. Melt the cheese until it barely drips off the sides of the bread. Remove the bread from the oven, let it cool, then wrap it in foil and refrigerate.

Game Day:

Take your soup and bread straight from your fridge to your cooler. At the stadium, heat the soup on your Coleman stove or Charbroil grill it in a heatproof cooking pot. When the soup begins to boil, remove it from the heat and place the foil containing the bread directly on the heat source. Once the cheese begins to melt, serve the soup in bowls topped with the floating cheese bread. Serves 6.

Serve with lots of extra french bread and a salad.

Burgundy Beef "Soup"

Here is a hearty beef stew that I've been cooking for over 25 years. I first made it in college and have resurrected it for cold weather tailgating.

Ingredients Required:

2 to 3 lbs. "good" cut of beef like chuck steak
¼ cup canola or olive oil
10 small onions
1 tsp. salt
one lb. large fresh mushrooms
1 bottle red wine

To Prepare:

Trim all fat from beef and cook it in hot stew pot. While fat is cooking, cut the beef into one inch squares. Remove fat hunks from the stew pot and put in oil and beef to brown (20 to 30 minutes). Peel onions enough to remove all outer skin, but not so much that they won't remain together during stewing. Add onions and salt to browned meat. Cover whole stew mixture with red wine (1 to 1½ cups). Simmer 30 minutes longer. Wash fresh mushrooms, trim off any bad parts and dry on paper towel. Cut mushrooms vertically into mushroom shaped slices. Add mushrooms to mixture. Use rest of wine to cover if necessary. If not, drink it at room temperature. Simmer 30 minutes longer. Take out one piece of meat and test it. If it is tender and full of the rich wine taste, the mixture is done. If the meat is a little tough, cook longer.

Serve in heavy duty bowls or mugs with thick pieces of french bread for dipping. Serves eight to ten.

This soup is delicious — my family loves it when I make it for a tailgate.

Barbecue Rib Tips

These easy ribs are a contribution from Rich Benassi, a Notre Dame fan who gave me a taste at a "cold weather" Irish game. Rich got the recipe years ago from Betty Dembinski, a co-worker and friend. The recipe is good for tailgaters because there is so little game day work involved.

Ingredients Required:

Oven, preheated to 300 degrees
2 slabs of pork rib tips
2 bottles of your favorite barbecue sauce
bottled water

Advance Preparations:

Ask your butcher for two slabs of pork rib tips. Then have him cut them across the bones in one inch strips. When you are ready to cook, cut these one inch strips about every two inches, making one by two inch pieces.

The Night Before:

Place the pieces of rib tips in a roaster pan. Mix one bottle of sauce and one bottle of water in a bowl. Pour over the rib tips in the roaster. Cover the roaster and bake for 45 minutes. Drain off $^2/_3$ of the sauce mixture. Baste the tops of the ribs with more barbecue sauce. Return the ribs to the oven, uncovered, for 20 minutes.

Leave these ribs in the roaster pan and refrigerate.

On Game Day:

Throw the ribs on the grill until warm! Serve with pasta or other salad and cold beer or pop.

Having fun at Rich's tailgate are (from upper left, clockwise) Matt Benassi, Jim Benassi, Mike Benassi, Crystal Koszyk, Nick Bartolini, Brian Szklarek, Chris Dutrieux, Rich Benassi and John Benassi

Italian Casserole

When the weather gets cold and damp, Phyllis Grossman serves this hot dish at Louisville games outside Cardinal Stadium. She stole the recipe from a friend in Pittsburgh, Kansas.

Ingredients Required:

1 8 oz. package spaghetti
1 10 oz. package frozen chopped spinach, thawed and drained
1 10 oz. can mushroom soup, undiluted
1 clove garlic, minced or pressed
$^1/_2$ tsp. dried whole marjoram
$^1/_2$ tsp. dried whole tarragon

$^1/_4$ tsp. salt (optional)
$^1/_4$ tsp. pepper
1 lb. Italian sausage
1 large onion, chopped
1 egg, slightly beaten
1 16 oz. carton of ricotta cheese
1 tomato, chopped
$^1/_3$ cup fresh parsley, chopped

The Night Before:

Cook and drain the spaghetti. Spread in a lightly greased 13 x 9" baking dish. Set aside. Combine spinach, mushroom soup, garlic, marjoram, tarragon, salt and pepper. Spoon mixture over spaghetti. Cook the sausage, without casing, over medium heat in a skillet with onion, stirring frequently to crumble the sausage. Drain well. Sprinkle over the spinach mixture. Combine the egg and ricotta cheese. Spread over sausage mixture. Cover the dish and chill at least eight hours.

Game Day:

Remove dish from refrigerator and let stand for 30 minutes. Preheat oven to 375 degrees. Bake at 375 degrees for 35 to 50 minutes. Sprinkle finished dish with chopped tomatoes and parsley.

Pictured left are Phyllis and her husband Stuart (center) tailgating with friends at Cardinal Stadium before a U of L game.

Breakfast Casserole

This breakfast casserole combines the taste of eggs, Canadian bacon and cheese in a manner similar to quiche — only better! Mary Dee Daily serves it at early (before noon start) Purdue games. She adapted the recipe from a Presbyterian church fund-raiser book. The Casserole is hearty and tasty!

Ingredients Required:

8 slices Pepperidge Farm white bread

8 oz. shredded Monterey Jack cheese

8 oz. Philadelphia cream cheese

4 oz. chopped green drained chili peppers

1 large package Canadian bacon

12 eggs

2 cups milk

½ teaspoon dry mustard

dash garlic salt

dash red pepper

1½ cup shredded cheddar cheese

To Prepare:

Preheat oven to 350 degrees. Cut the bread into cubes including the crust. Arrange evenly in a greased, shallow three quart casserole dish. Sprinkle with Monterey Jack, cheddar and cream cheese. Top with chili peppers. In a large bowl, beat eggs until mixed. Stir in milk, mustard, red pepper and garlic salt. Pour mixture over casserole mix, cover with foil and refrigerate overnight. Bake uncovered in oven for 50 minutes or until knife inserted near center comes out clean.

Serve with fruit and crescent butter rolls stuffed with peach or apple butter before baking.

Our hungry tailgaters are (from left to right) Mary Helen Stout, Carl Hynds, Mary Dee Daily and Michael J. Daily

Tailgate Lasagna

This lasagna has been developed by my wife Cindy, from a recipe she got from Jane Orwig, wife of the former Indiana Athletic Director, Bill Orwig. The pepperoni gives it a spicy pizza flavor.

Ingredients required:

12 slices lasagna noodles
1 lb. ground seasoned sausage (any variety)
1 large can pitted black olives, sliced
2 15 oz. cartons ricotta cheese
24 oz. shredded mozzarella cheese
72 oz. of your favorite spaghetti sauce or pizza sauce

18 oz. bag frozen spinach
4 cloves garlic, peeled and chopped
1½ tbsp. dried oregano
¾ tbsp. dried basil
2 eggs
1 tbsp. course salt
fresh ground pepper to taste

To Prepare:

Boil lasagna noodles approximately eight minutes, drain and place on waxed paper to cool. Brown sausage and drain well.

Drain all the water from spinach, press it frequently. Slice black olives. Mix together rictta cheese, eggs, garlic, oregano, basil, salt and pepper. Preheat oven to 325 degrees and then grease 9 x 13" casserole and layer ingredients as follows:

1. Use sauce to cover the bottom of the dish, followed by four noodles to cover sauce. Cover with one half the ricotta cheese mixture and spread spinach over ricotta. Cover the spinach with olives and then mozzarella.

2. Spread sauce over the mozzarella and cover with four lasagna noodles. Over this spread the remaining ricotta mixture. Spread cooked sausage over ricotta and cover sausage with pepperoni. Mozzarella is used to cover pepperoni.

3. Add sauce to cover the mozzarella and cover the sauce with the remaining noodles. Cover over with more sauce and coat all with final layer of mozzarella.

Cover entire dish with foil and bake at 325 for one hour. After first 45 minutes, uncover the lasagna so that it will brown.

Side Dish Survey: Warm Weather

What is your favorite side dish for warm weather tailgating? Almost 200 tailgaters were interviewed over a two year period at ten stadiums. There were 121 replies to this question.

Choice	Number	Percent
1. Chips and Dip	31	20
2. Salads	27	18
3. Potato Salad	24	16
4. Veggies	18	12
5. Cheese & Beans (tie)	11 (ea.)	7
7. Fruit	7	5
8. Wings, Nuts, pretzels & deviled eggs (4-way tie)	3 (ea.)	2

Potato Chips & Crackers

The potato chip was a relatively recent discovery. George Crumb, the chef at a famous dining room at Saratoga Springs, New York in the late 1800s, came up with his potato chip invention to please a finicky customer. This fellow kept sending his potato strips back to the kitchen because he felt they needed a more refined look. Crumb finally sliced the potato so thin that he was left with a chip he fried in fat. The customer was delighted. From that elegant dining room, the potato chip swept America. Where would the modern tailgater be without them?

Crackers are basically flour and water, baked and dried. They date back to the Roman soldiers where they were called biscuits. Ship's cooks used them as a food staple and called them hardtack. It is said that even the great Christopher Columbus brought them along on his trip to the Americas.

In 1794 the first U.S. cracker bakery was established in Newburyport, Massachusetts. In 1840 machines were invented to mass produce crackers. However, it wasn't until the gold rush of 1849 that crackers became popular in this country. These early prospectors clambered for crackers because they lasted a long time without spoiling, and they tasted good.

Chili Dip

Linda Cunningham, a William Jewel College fan, makes this chili dip
to serve with chips. Mizzou tailgaters love it too. She got the recipe in
Tulsa at the Woodbine Bunko Club.

Ingredients Required:

1 16 oz. can chili without beans
8 oz. sour cream
8 oz. cream cheese

To Prepare:

Heat together until smooth. Use corn chips, tortilla chips or whatever
you like as dippers.

Award-Winning Tailgate Caviar Dipper

Karen Nichols, a '74 Purdue grad, won Purdue's National Tailgating
Contest with this great dipping appetizer. This recipe appears courtesy of the Purdue Alumnus magazine.

Ingredients Required:

Dip:

3 16 oz. cans black-eyed peas
2 medium ripe tomatoes, diced
1 green bell pepper, seeded and
   diced
6 green onions, chopped
¾ cup green olives, diced
2 jalapeno peppers, minced and
.   seeded - if desired

Dressing:

¼ cup olive oil
2 tbsp. medium salsa
2 tbsp. lemon juice
1 tbsp. Dijon mustard
2 cloves garlic, minced
1 tsp. salt
1 tsp. dried thyme
1 tsp. sugar
½ tsp. hot pepper sauce

The Night Before:

Drain peas; place in a large bowl. Add tomatoes, pepper, onions, olives and jalapeno peppers to peas. In a separate bowl, combine all
dressing ingredients. Pour over pea mixture and mix thoroughly.

Game Day:

Refrigerate overnight or at least two hours. Serve with tortillas or corn
chips.

Chili Con Queso

Hot and loaded with character, this dip is great with a beer, corn chips or anything else while you're waiting for the burgers and brats to cook. The recipe is from Indiana fan Connie La Brash, whose husband John loves this dip in cold weather. Connie says not to substitute for the Old El Paso ingredients. She's tried it and it's just not the same.

Ingredients Required:

2 lbs. Velveeta cheese
1 lb. hot pork sausage
1 can Old El Paso tomatoes and chilies
1 can Old El Paso chopped chilies

To Prepare:

Melt the cheese in a double boiler or microwave. Fry the sausage and then drain well. Add sausage and other ingredients to the cheese and stir. Keep this dish warm.

Serve with tortilla chips, crackers, veggies or even bread sticks.

Taco Pizza Dip

Fans at Purdue games are lucky because they get great creations like Marjorie Silvey's Taco Pizza Dip. This is a dip which looks and tastes like a taco pizza. Just grab a corn chip, or any other chip for that matter, and enjoy! Marjorie got this recipe from her niece to give luck to the Boilermakers against Indiana and Notre Dame.

Ingredients Required:

1 8 oz. pkg. soft Philadelphia Cream Cheese
1 cup catsup (or mild taco sauce)
½ cup bacon bits
1 tsp. horseradish
finely chopped tomatoes, green peppers and green onions
shredded cheeses

To Prepare:

Spread cream cheese on a pizza-style pan to resemble crust of a pizza. Combine the catsup, bacon bits and horseradish. Spread over the cheese to resemble pizza sauce. Add chopped veggies as a pizza topping. Sprinkle with cheese. Refrigerate until serving.

Lemon Creme Fruit Dip

Luci O'Donnell, a Boston College fan from St. Louis, makes this fruit dip.

Ingredients Required:

2 eggs
$^1/_3$ cup lemon juice
$^1/_2$ cup water
1 cup sugar
1 tbsp. cornstarch
1 tsp. vanilla
1 cup whipped cream

To Prepare:

Combine ½ cup sugar, water and cornstarch in a pan. Heat until thickened; remove from heat and gradually beat in the mixture of eggs, the remainder of the sugar   and lemon juice. Cook over low heat, stir until slightly thickened. Remove from heat, and add vanilla. Allow the mixture to cool. Fold in whipped cream. Serve with fresh fruit. Good with apple slices, pears, berries, melons and more.

Vegetable Dip

Penn State tailgates are blessed with a great veggie dip by Donna Swankanski. She got the recipe from her sister and serves it in warm weather with all sorts of vegetables.

Ingredients Required:

¾ cup sour cream
¾ cup mayonnaise
1 tbsp. dehydrated onion
1 tbsp. parsley flakes
1 tbsp. Lawrey's Seasoned Salt
1 tsp. dillweed

To Prepare:

Mix the mayo and sour cream in a Rubbermaid container. Add the other ingredients, stir and chill.

Pasta Salad

Here are a couple of pasta salads which are well received at tailgates and for that late night snack watching football replays and scores. The author picked up a variation of this recipe at a Texas game, but has made substantial changes to it over the past few years. Make this as a Ranch or Italian salad flavor.

Ranch Flavor

Ingredients Required:

1 package powdered ranch party/ chip dip (not salad dressing)
1 cup sour cream
1 cup milk
1 pound Rotini or Rotelli

3 cups assorted fresh vegetables (green or red peppers, radishes, or celery, for example)
1 cup large, pitted, ripe olives

To Prepare:

Prepare the party dip with the sour cream and milk per instructions. Let the mixture thicken in the refrigerator (often an hour or longer). Prepare pasta per package instructions or drop pasta into an eight quart pot of boiling water pre-sprayed with cooking oil. Cook eight to ten minutes until done al dente. Test by spearing a chunk with a fork and eating it. Drain the pasta. While pasta drains, prepare olives and veggies. Wash veggies in cold water and chop into bite size pieces. Drain large olives, then slice each in half, lengthwise. Put the pasta in a large Rubbermaid canister. Mix in all ingredients including the dip. Put the lid on and chill the entire mixture overnight.

Serve this salad with cold or hot sandwiches. The ranch dip gives it a little bite. This will provide more than a dozen big servings.

Italian Flavor

Ingredients Required:

1 pound package pasta
3 cups fresh vegetables
1 cup large pitted ripe olives
3 tbsp. chopped parsley

2 tbsp. Dijon mustard
½ tsp. fresh ground pepper
16 oz. bottle of your favorite Italian salad dressing

To Prepare:

Prepare the pasta, drain, combine the ingredients just as above. This dish can be thickened with sour cream.

Mom's BLT Pasta Salad

Here is a great pasta salad developed by Carey Clarke Aron for Tennessee games at Knoxville. The Aron's own The Pasta Shoppe in Nashville, which sells those Collegiate Licensed Pastas.

Ingredients Required:
2 6 oz. bags collegiate pasta
½ green pepper finely chopped
3 medium tomatoes, diced and drained
¾-1 lb. bacon, crumbled
½ cup mayonnaise
½ tsp. salt
¼ tsp. pepper

To Prepare:
Cook pasta as directed, drain and rinse with cold water. Add remaining ingredients and season to taste. If you are making this ahead of
time, add the bacon just before serving to maintain crispness. Enjoy!
Serves 6-8.

*Pictured are 'Bama and war Eagle
pasta from The Pasta Shoppe's
collection of over 40 officially licensed
pastas. These uniquely shaped
ingredients make the consummate
pasta salad for a tailgater who wants
everything to be perfect, including the
pasta. Fans can call The Pasta Shoppe
direct at (800) 247-0188 or find their
local school pasta at their favorite
specialty store.*

Top Ten Pasta Schools*

1. Tennessee
2. Auburn
3. Alabama
4. Indiana

5. Kentucky
6. Notre Dame
7. Michigan

8. Florida
9. Penn State
10. Florida State

*The above rankings are derived from sales figures from The Pasta Shoppe. Fans from these colleges lead the nation in serving licensed pasta.

Caesar Salad

This recipe was given to me by my friend Dick Truxel, a '63 graduate of Penn State. For more info on the Truxels, refer back to the sad incident of the cheeseburger soup.

Ingredients Required:

1 can anchovies (flat fillets)
8 oz. olive oil
5 cloves garlic (about ½ bulb)
1 egg
4 oz. Romano cheese (grated)

4 heads Romaine lettuce
worchestershire sauce
ground pepper
1 lemon
croutons

To Prepare:

Using a garlic press, squeeze garlic into wooden salad bowl and put in pulp from the press as well. Rub the garlic oil and pulp over the entire inner surface of bowl, then discard the pulp. Cut lemon in half and squeeze one half into bowl. Add the chopped anchovies, olive oil, raw egg, ¾ of the cheese, several shakes of Worchestershire sauce and some ground pepper. Stir well and scrape over the insides of the bowl. Let stand for at least half an hour.

When ready to serve, shred the lettuce and mash it with your hands (this breaks down the heavy veins in the lettuce and makes its juices flow). Toss the entire salad by hand and scrunch and squeeze the lettuce while doing so. Squeeze the remaining half of the lemon over the top of the salad, sprinkle the remaining cheese over the dish and top with croutons. Serves 6.

Dick and Linda Truxel

Award-Winning Country Coleslaw

Mary Kudrak Short, a Texas resident who graduated from Purdue in
'88, won the Purdue National Tailgating Contest with this great slaw.
This recipe appears courtesy of the *Purdue Alumnus* magazine.

Ingredients Required:

$^1/_2$ cup mayonnaise
2 tbsp. sugar
2 tbsp. cider vinegar
$^3/_4$ tbsp. salt
$^1/_2$ tsp. mustard
$^1/_8$ tsp. celery seeds
4 cups shredded cabbage
$^3/_4$ cup diced green pepper
2 tbsp. sliced green onions

To Prepare:

In a large bowl, stir together the first six ingredients. Add remaining
ingredients and toss well. Cover and chill.

Chinese Coleslaw

Molly Jones, a Culver-Stockton fan, makes this great coleslaw as a
salad dish for tailgaters.

Ingredients:

Slaw:
1 lb. chopped cabbage with carrots
5 oz. sunflower nuts
2 green onions chopped
2 packages Ramen noodles (chicken)
Dressing:
$^1/_3$ cup vinegar
$^1/_2$ cup sugar
$^1/_2$ cup salad oil
2 packages soup seasoning from Ramen noodles

To Prepare:

Mix dressing and set aside in one Rubbermaid container. Mix slaw in
another large container. Dress right before serving at your tailgate.

Deviled Eggs

Mary Ellen C. Van Buskirk, Purdue '57, has been tailgating during three different decades. She lives in western Illinois, but treks with friends to Purdue's home games. Her tailgates have been featured in newspaper and books. She gave us this deviled egg recipe because she always brings these eggs to the games, but never takes any home. Everybody loves them

Ingredients Required:

  1 dozen large eggs
  mayonnaise
  horseradish mustard
  Worcestershire sauce
  salt
  pepper
  black olives (for garnish)

To Prepare:

Boil one dozen large eggs. Cool and peel. Cut in half lengthwise. Remove the yokes to a bowl. Place the whites on a tray. Use a fork to mash the yokes adding mayonnaise, horseradish mustard, a dash of Worcestershire sauce, salt and pepper. This mixture should be soft like icing. Put filling back into the whites. Use a pastry tube if you'd like to be fancy. Garnish with a slice of black olive.

Chill these eggs in the refrigerator and keep cold until 30 minutes before serving.

Along with her great deviled eggs, Mary Ellen has a tradition of serving specially decorated cupcakes — these are decorated for both Northwestern and Purdue and shared with Northwestern grad, Ollie Grimm

Layered Ham Cubes

This great ham and cheese appetizer started at a pot luck group. Jean Milonski, a Southern Illinois fan, and my aunt gave us the recipe.

Ingredients Required:

2 tbsp. mayonnaise
2 tbsp. horseradish sauce
1 tsp. worchestershire sauce
½ tsp. salt
8 oz. package cream cheese
6 thin, oblong slices of ham

To Prepare:

Blend all ingredients except ham. Put a slice of ham on waxed paper. Cover ham with cheese mixture. Repeat procedure, making six layers. Wrap in foil and freeze for at least two hours. Remove one hour before serving. Cut into 24 squares and spear with toothpicks to serve.

Side Dish Survey: Cold Weather

What is your favorite side dish for cold weather tailgating? Almost 200 tailgaters were interviewed over a two year period at ten stadiums. There were 94 replies to this question.

Choice	Number	Percent
1. Baked Beans	23	20
2. Chips & dips	22	19
3. Chili	9	8
4. Cheese	8	7
5. Potato Salad, Pizza & Salad (3-way tie)	6 (ea.)	5
8. Corn & Soup (tie)	4 (ea.)	2
9. Pretzels & Deviled Eggs (tie)	3 (ea.)	2

Italian Baked Beans — Fagiolo Italiano

Richmond, Indiana's Ron De Mao, a PGA Master Pro, says "man cannot live by golf alone." For hungry football fans, he fixes Fagiolo Italiano. The recipe has evolved from Pitt Panther tailgates. He claims they were instrumental in a national championship football season for the University of Pittsburgh.

Ingredients Required:

1 medium onion, chopped
¼ lb. bacon, diced
1 green pepper, chopped
1 clove garlic, chopped

1 6 lb. can Van Camps Pork and Beans
1 cup brown sugar
1 cup catsup

To Prepare:

Saute bacon, onions, green pepper and garlic in olive oil over low heat until vegetables are cooked. Preheat oven to 350 degrees. Pour bacon mixture into large casserole dish. Add beans, brown sugar, catsup and season with salt and pepper to individual taste. Bake at 350 for 90 minutes.

Baked Potato Salad

This is the best hot potato salad I ever tasted. Linda McNeil uses this dish at Iowa Hawkeye games as an accompaniment to brats or other grilled sandwiches. She says, "When the weather gets colder, Hot Potato Salad is a hit!"

Ingredients Required:

8 cooked, peeled and diced
   potatoes
1 lb. Velveeta cheese, diced
1 cup salad dressing

$^1/_3$ cup bacon bits
$^1/_2$ cup chopped onion
4 tsp. instant chicken bullion
3 hard boiled eggs, chopped

To Prepare:

Toss all ingredients together and place them into a buttered baking dish. Bake at 325 degrees for one hour. Or make the casserole and refrigerate overnight. Then bake before leaving for the game. Allow 4 minutes longer if ingredients are refrigerated.

Serve with grilled meats, dill pickles and cold beverages.

Dessert Survey: Warm Weather

What is your favorite dessert for warm weather tailgating? Almost 200 tailgaters were interviewed over a two year period at ten stadiums. There were 82 replies to this question.

Choice	Number	Percent
1. Bars	36	42
2. Cookies	22	26
3. Fruit	11	13
4. Cake	9	10
5. Pie	4	5

Dessert Survey: Cold Weather

What is your favorite dessert for cold weather tailgating? Almost 200 tailgaters were interviewed over a two year period at ten stadiums. There were 66 replies to this question.

Choice	Number	Percent
1. Bars	30	43
2. Cookies	17	25
3. Cake	9	13
4. Pie	4	6
4. Fruit	4	6
6. Candy	2	4

Something Sweet

Dessert is defined as the last course of a meal. It is traditionally a sweet course with French origins. Desservir, a very early French word (1700s) meant to clear the table. The word "dessert" comes from this word, although now it means that which comes after the last course.

To trace the history of desserts, you probably have to go back as far as possible in time. The first man tasting fruit could be classified as a dessert eater, at least if he ended his meal with it. The early Egyptians baked a lot of foods made with wheat. By adding sweets like honey or figs, they had a cake. Sugar, however, was a product of the Americas. It was first brought to Europe by Columbus.

That's when Europe discovered its sweet tooth.

During the Renaissance it became fashionable for the wealthy to indulge in cakes, pies, chocolate and other rich, sweet desserts. It was a status symbol for a noble to serve sweets.

Today's desserts are an evolution from the diet of those "old country" nobility. Tailgaters notoriously love their sweets. After all, as we said earlier, the game only comes once a week, why not splurge? Tailgaters, however, strive to find desserts which are easy to eat and store. If a dish is sweet and can be held in you hands, you'll find it in a college football parking lot on Saturday.

The Bar
(Cookie)

Probably one of the easiest, best tasting, homemade desserts a tailgater can serve, "the bar", became almost a cult dessert in the 80's for fans of the radio show called "A Prairie Home Companion". The show's host, Garrison Keillor, and one of its creative geniuses Howard Mohr, have canonized this dish as the "native dessert" of Minnesota. Their fans know that bars should always be served with a "little lunch" — the name affectionately given to the heavy snack eaten three to five times a day by Minnesotans.

Most "Middle Americans", however, have eaten bars all their life. We start out with those chewy Rice Crispy marshmallow bars in school and scouts. Every home and all churches serve brownies which can qualify as a bar. And at Christmas time, you always run across those fruit and nut squares so small that you eat about 10 at a time; these are bars too. So maybe it's prudent that someone define the word "bar".

A bar is a section of a desert. Bars are made in a pan, cut into serving size squares or rectangles. Bars don't have to be baked, but most are. They are sweet and easy. Some are frosted, some are like cookies, but all must be able to be eaten with your hands. Leftover bars are great when the tailgater has returned home and is looking for a "little lunch" (that late snack) while watching ESPN's Saturday Night Football.

The evolution of bars surely came through the need or desire to save time. Instead of making cookies with the rolling, cutting, baking sheets and cooling, someone decided to make it all in a pan and cut it into cookies later. Some bars require two portion baking to vary texture and toppings, but they all cool right in the baking pan with a minimum of mess. Bars can be lightly sweetened like a coffee cake or they can be as rich as candy. They allow for the creativity of the cook.

Butterscotch Brownies (Bars)

"A good friend always made these brownies for my birthday," says Brent Kelsey, an Indiana fan. "She would freeze them in freezer bags so you could take a piece out individually and enjoy. We started taking them to IU games because they were so convenient and tasty."

Ingredients Required:

¼ cup butter
1 cup light brown sugar, packed
1 egg
¾ cup flour
1 tsp. baking powder
½ tsp. salt
½ tsp. vanilla
½ cup chopped walnuts

To Prepare:

Preheat oven to 350 degrees. Melt butter over low heat. Remove from heat and stir in brown sugar until it is well-blended. Cool the mixture. Stir in the egg. Sift together flour, baking powder and salt, then stir into the mixture. Add the vanilla and nuts and stir together.

Spread mix into an eight-inch square baking dish/pan. Bake at 350 for approximately 25 minutes. When they are done, only a slight imprint remains when touched lightly with a finger. Don't overbake. Cut into bars when warm.

You Need This Book!

Recommended reading for all tailgate chefs, *A to Z Bar Cookies* by Marie Simmons is a handy reference for easy-to-make delicious bars. It sells for $12.95 and is published by Chapters Books of Shelburne, Vermont.

BAR COOKIES
A to Z
By Marie Simmons

Photographs by Susan Marie Anderson

Cinnamon Bars

Minnesota is the home of "the bar," and Ronda Thierer serves these bars with coffee. They are great for a late morning tailgate.

Ingredients Required:

2 cups flour
1¼ cups granulated sugar
¼ cup brown sugar
½ cup soft margarine
1 tsp. baking soda
1 tsp. cinnamon
¾ tsp. salt

1 cup buttermilk
1 tsp. vanilla
1 egg
1 cup powdered sugar
3 tbsp. milk
¼ tsp. almond extract

To Prepare:

Preheat oven to 350 degrees.

To prepare bars: combine flour, granulated sugar and soft margarine. Mix on low until crumbly. Press two cups of this mixture into an ungreased 9 x 13" pan. To the rest of the mixture, add the soda, cinnamon, salt, buttermilk, vanilla and egg. Blend well and pour over pressed portion. Bake at 350 for 20 minutes. Cool for 20 minutes before frosting.

To prepare frosting: blend the powdered sugar, almond extract and enough milk to make it spreadable.

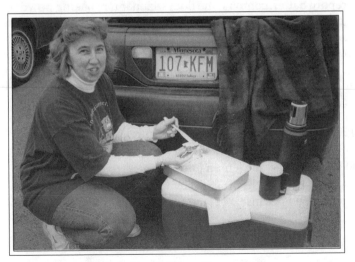

Ronda and her delicious Cinnamon Bars

Carrot-Pecan Bars
(Carrot Cake in a Bar)

Marie Simmons, in her book *A to Z Bar Cookies*, explains that she created this recipe from her favorite carrot cake. She says, "It took a couple of experiments before the transformation from cake to bar was complete, but it certainly was worth the effort." She recommends using fresh grated nutmeg in the frosting if possible.

Ingredients Required:

Cake:
- 1 cup unbleached all-purpose flour
- ½ cup whole wheat flour
- 1 tsp. ground cinnamon
- ½ tsp. baking powder
- ½ tsp. salt
- ½ cup finely chopped pecans
- ¾ cup vegetable oil
- 1 cup packed light brown sugar
- 2 large eggs
- 1 tsp. vanilla extract
- 2 cups carrots, cut into ½ inch pieces

Frosting:
- 2 3 oz. packages cream cheese, softened
- 1 cup confectioners' sugar, sifted
- 1 tbsp. fresh lemon juice
- ½ tsp. freshly grated nutmeg
- ½ tsp. vanilla extract
- 2 tbsp. finely chopped pecans

To Prepare:

Preheat oven to 350 degrees. Lightly butter a 13 x 9" baking pan.

To prepare batter: combine the flours, cinnamon, baking powder, nutmeg and salt in a large bowl; add the pecans; stir to blend. Place the oil, brown sugar, eggs and vanilla in the bowl of a food processor. Process until blended. With the motor running, gradually add the carrots through the feed tube. Process until the carrots are finely chopped. Pour the carrot mixture over the dry ingredients and stir until well-blended. Spread the batter in the prepared pan. Bake for 35 minute, or until the edges pull away from the sides of the pan. Cool on a wire rack.

To prepare frosting: beat the cream cheese and confectioner's sugar until smooth. Add the lemon juice, nutmeg and vanilla.

Final step: Spread the frosting over the cooled bars. Sprinkle with finely chopped pecans. Let stand for one hour before cutting into bars.

No Bake Butterfinger Bars

A real sweet treat, these bars are for those candy lovers who are embarrassed to carry candy bars to the tailgate. Ronda Thierer of Minnesota fixes 'em for the kid in all of us.

Ingredients Required:

4 cups crushed graham crackers
2 cups powdered sugar
1 cup peanut butter
1 cup melted margarine
1 cup chocolate chips, melted

To Prepare:

Mix grahams, sugar and peanut butter. Add the melted margarine and press into ungreased 9 x 13" baking pan. Top with melted chocolate chips. Cool and cut into bars.

Chocolate Bars

This recipe was passed on to Teddy Hite a few years ago by her aunt. Teddy says it's a big hit at all Penn State Games.

Ingredients Required:

1 package German Chocolate cake mix
¾ cup margarine
1 cup chopped nuts
14 oz. package light caramels
1 cup chocolate chips
5 oz. evaporated milk

To Prepare:

Preheat oven to 350 degrees. Combine caramels and one third of the evaporated milk. Melt slowly and set aside. In separate pan, melt margarine slowly and combine with the cake mix. Add the nuts and remaining evaporated milk. Stir by hand until the dough holds together like fudge.

Spread half the dough into a greased 9 x 13" baking dish. Bake at 350 for six minutes. Sprinkle the chocolate chips over the six minute crust. Drizzle the melted caramel over the chips. Dot the rest of the cake mix dough over the top. Return to the oven and bake 20 minutes longer. Cool and cut into bars.

Mandarin Orange Bars

These bars are a great warm weather dessert because they are sweet, but with the citrus taste of oranges. Shirley Wilmot serves them in Minnesota to other gopher fans.

Ingredients Required:

$^3/_4$ cup butter
$1^1/_2$ cups brown sugar
2 eggs
$1^1/_2$ cups flour
1 tsp. baking powder
$^1/_8$ tsp. salt
1 cup drained mandarin oranges (save liquid)
$^2/_3$ cup pecans or walnuts
2 cups powdered sugar

To Prepare:

Preheat oven to 350 degrees.

To prepare batter: Beat $^1/_2$ cup butter, brown sugar and eggs for 3 minutes. Then mix in flour, baking powder, salt, oranges and nuts. Bake in 9 x 13" baking dish in oven for 30 minutes or until done.

To prepare frosting: Mix powdered sugar with the rest of the batter. Then beat in mandarin orange juice a little at a time until frosting is the spreading consistency you like.

Coffee and bars are all Shirley packs in her cooler

Sticky Pecan Bars
(Pecan Pie in a Bar)

Another fantastic Marie Simmons recipe from her famous book, *A to Z Bar Cookies*, is this one for pecan bars. These bars are fashioned after her favorite pecan tart recipe

Ingredients Required:

Crust:
   1½ cups unbleached all-purpose flour
   ¼ cup sugar
   pinch of salt
   10 tbsp. (1 stick plus 2 tbsp.) cold unsalted butter, cut into pieces
   1 large egg yolk

Filling:
   ½ cup packed light brown sugar
   2 tbsp. unbleached all-purpose flours
   ¾ cup dark corn syrup
   3 large eggs
   1 tsp. vanilla extract
   2 cups large pecan halves

To Prepare:

Preheat oven to 400 degrees. Lightly butter a 9 x 13" square pan.

To prepare crust: Combine the flour, sugar and salt in the bowl of a food processor. With motor running, gradually add the butter through the feed tube; process until blended. Add the egg yolk and process until blended. Turn into the prepared pan and gather the dough together. Flatten with your hand and press evenly into the bottom of the pan, forming a ¼-inch edge up the sides of the pan. Refrigerate until ready to bake.

To prepare filling: In a medium-sized bowl, stir the brown sugar and flour until blended. Add the corn syrup, eggs and vanilla, whisk until well-blended. Spread the pecans in an even layer over the crust. Pour the filling over the top.

Bake for 10 minutes. Reduce the oven temperature to 350 degrees and bake for 25 minutes, or until the filling is firm. Cool on a wire rack before cutting into bars.

Crescent Cookies (Sandies)

These tasty powdered sugar crescents made by my mother, Bozena Milonska Drozda, are probably the best cookies I've ever tasted. She shipped these treats to all our relatives who served in WW II, Korea and Vietnam. They have been sent to Europe to relatives not as fortunate as the American wing of her family. She has probably sent out thousands of these cookies in the past 60 years.

Although her own tailgating days (Washington University) were over by 1935, she graciously has agreed to share these recipe with tailgaters of today.

Ingredients Required:

1 cup butter
½ cup confectioner's sugar
1 tsp. vanilla
2 cups flour
1 cup chopped pecans

To Prepare:

Cream butter and sugar. Add vanilla, flour and nuts. Mix into a dough. Shape small pieces of dough into crescents and place on an ungreased cookie sheet. Refrigerate for 30 minutes. Bake at 350 degrees for about 20 minutes. While still hot, roll the crescents in powdered sugar. Let the cookies cool and then wrap individually in small rectangles of waxed paper and foil.

The Right Candy

The art of offical licensing is not limited to hard goods and clothing. Now you can buy chocolates with the official team logo. Pictured are Hoosiers and Nuts for IU. These delicious confections are products of the South Bend (Indiana) Chocolate Company, who also make Rocknes and Domers for Notre Dame fans.

These chocolates, soon to be available for many other colleges are a great touch for a fancy tailgate party. Football and chocolate fans can call (800) 301-4961 for ordering information.

Peanut Butter Cup Cookies

Sally Pietrzak brings these great-tasting cookies to almost every Notre Dame home game. She says they are a takeoff of the Hershey's Kisses cookies.

Ingredients Required:

1¾ cup flour	1 egg
1 tsp. baking soda	2 tbsp. milk
½ tsp. salt	1 cup sugar
½ cup brown sugar	1 tsp. vanilla
½ cup shortening	48 bite-sized Reese's peanut butter
½ cup peanut butter	cups (refrigerate until used)

To Prepare:

Combine all ingredients except Reese's cups and regular sugar and mix until dough is smooth. Form mixture into approximately 48 balls; roll balls in sugar. Bake 10-12 minutes. Remove the baking sheet from the oven and place a peanut butter cup on each cookie and press down until the cookie cracks.

Makes four dozen.

Enjoying Sally's peanut butter cup cookies are (from left to right) Tom Biggs, David Czajkowski, John Michalski, Sally and Gloria Michalski.

Undra's Graham Cracker Cake and Vanilla Cream Frosting

Undra Johnson, a West Virginia Mountaineer, also played professional football with the Falcons, Saints, San Antonio Riders of the WFL, and, in 1995, the Dallas Cowboys. His recipe also comes from *All-Pro Recipes.*

Ingredients Required:

Cake:

    1 cup flour
    1 heaping cup sugar
    3½ tsp. baking powder
    ¾ tsp. salt
    ¾ cup shortening
    2 cups crushed graham crackers
    1 cup + 2 tsp. milk
    1½ tsp. vanilla
    2 eggs, beaten

Frosting:

    ½ cup butter
    3½ cups sifted confectioners' sugar
    5 tbsp. light cream
    1tsp. vanilla extract

To Prepare:

Preheat oven to 375 degrees. Mix all dry cake ingredients together until well-blended. Add shortening and mix well. This will make a lumpy mixture. Fold in milk, vanilla and eggs. Beat with an electric mixer for about three minutes. Pour the entire mixture into a greased and floured 9 x 13" cake pan. Bake 30-35 minutes.

After you have removed cake from the oven and given it ample time to cool, it is time to make the frosting. Lightly brown butter in a small sklllet over low heat. Remove from heat. Combine butter sugar, light cream and vanilla in medium mixing bowl. Beat with electric mixer until mixture is smooth and fluffy. Spread evenly over completely cooled cake. Serves 10.

Apple Cake

Joan Crocket baked this tasty apple cake every Friday during high school football season for her son's team, who thought it was a good luck charm. She serves it at Ohio State games on Saturdays.

Ingredients Required:

3 eggs	1 tsp. cinnamon
1¾ cups sugar	1 tsp. baking soda
1 cup cooking oil	½ tsp. salt
1 tsp. vanilla	2 cups chopped or sliced apples
2 cups flour	1 cup chopped nuts

To Prepare:

Preheat oven to 350. Beat the eggs, sugar, oil and vanilla. Sift flour, cinnamon, soda and salt into the wet mixture and mix well. Stir in apples and nuts and mix again. Pour into a greased floured 9 x 13" baking pan. Bake at 350 degrees for 50 to 60 minutes. Sprinkle with powdered sugar when cool.

Pineapple Cream Cake

Louis Riddick loaned us this recipe from *All-Pro Recipes*. Louis is a former Thorpe Award Finalist, provost scholar and dean's list student at Pitt. He went on to play in the NFL with the 49ers, Falcons and Browns. He is the founder of the Hit the Books pro-education campaign.

Ingredients Required:

Cake:
- 1 16 oz. can crushed pineapple (undrained)
- 2 cups sugar
- 2 cups flour
- 2 eggs
- 1 cup nuts
- 2 tsp. baking soda

1 tsp. vanilla

Icing:
- ¾ stick butter
- 8 oz. cream cheese
- 1½ cup confectioners' sugar
- 1 tsp. vanilla
- 1 cup crushed walnuts or almonds

To Prepare:

Preheat oven to 350 degrees. Beat all cake ingredients until well-mixed. Bake in a 9 x 13" glass pan for 45 minutes or until center is set. Begin preparing icing. Beat all icing ingredients together until they are spreadable. Spread over lukewarm cake and sprinkle with nuts.

Award-Winning Dirt Dessert

Robin Paris Baele, an Arizona resident who graduated from Purdue in 1981, won the Purdue National Tailgating Contest with this great dessert. This recipe appears courtesy of the Purdue Alumnus magazine.

Ingredients Required:

8 oz. cream cheese
1 cup powdered sugar
¼ cup margarine
2 small packages instant vanilla pudding
2¾ cups milk
1 large (3 row) package Oreo cookies
12 oz. Cool Whip

For Fun:

plastic flower pot
spade
silk flowers (in school colors)
plastic spider
gummi worms

To Prepare:

Combine cream cheese, sugar and margarine. Mix pudding and milk in separate bowl. Combine cream cheese mixture with the pudding mixture. Fold in Cool Whip. Crush one row of Oreos in food processor until white is gone. Put aluminium foil or waxed paper in bottom of pot. Line with one row of crushed cookie crumbs, spoon in half of the creamy mixture. Add another row of crushed cookie crumbs, add the rest of the creamy mixture, then add the last layer of crushed Oreo crumbs. Freeze until firm.

To serve this tailgate center-piece, thaw and then put in flowers. Stick the spade into the pot. Put the spider on the flowers and drape the pot with gummi worms. It looks unique and tastes great. You will need bowls or plates and forks or spoons.

Butterfinger Delight Cake

Elenore Porter serves this great, very sweet dessert. The most common question from most of her neighboring Minnesota fans is "Is this a cake or is it candy?"

Ingredients Required:

8 Butterfinger candy bars (crushed)
1 angel food cake cut into pieces
1 pint whipping cream
2 cups powdered sugar
½ cup melted butter

To Prepare:

Put cake pieces in 9 x 12" pan. Whip cream until it peaks. In a second bowl, mix butter and powdered sugar. Combine with whip cream and spread evenly over the cake pieces. Sprinkle crushed butterfingers over the top. Refrigerate. It should be served cold.

The Bar
(not the cookie)

Since the stadium parking lot is miles away from their kitchen, liquor cabinet or favorite spirit store, there is no crime in the tailgater organizer taking drink orders a few days in advance. In fact, it is perfectly acceptable for someone to put their drink order in when they RSVP an invitation to a tailgate party. Bar space is limited, and everyone understands the necessity of bringing only the most important drink fixtures.

Usually regular tailgaters drink the same things week after week anyway. At least they do in similar weather. A person who likes beer will prefer it through the whole season, changing only to a hot drink if the weather is really cold. Serious martini drinkers probably like them in most weather. And, an avid coffee drinker will take a cup anytime. The key is to get to know the people who will be with you. Or better yet, let everyone bring their own drinks (BYOB).

People who are very particular about what they drink are probably happier if they take care of themselves. If they want a certain gin and vermouth mixture, let them do it right. If they have access to something they feel is special, let them bring it and pass it around.

A wise practice for a tailgating party is to split the responsibility for parts of the menu among the participants. By doing this, no one

Beverage Survey: Warm Weather

What is your favorite drink for warm weather tailgating? Almost 200 tailgaters were interviewed over a two year period at ten stadiums. There were 128 replies to this question.

Choice	Number	Percent
1. Beer	81	64
2. Mixed Drinks	24	19
3. Soft Drinks	20	15
4. Other	3	2

Beverage Survey: Cold Weather

What is your favorite drink for cold weather tailgating? Almost 200 tailgaters were interviewed over a two year period at ten stadiums. There were 131 replies to this question.

Choice	Number	Percent
1. Beer	60	46
2. Mixed Drinks	28	22
3. Coffee	20	15
4. Hot Chocolate	11	8
5. Soft Drinks	10	8
4. Other	2	1

person gets stuck bringing too much and everyone gets to contribute. In this type of party, one person can be assigned to bring soft drinks and maybe beer (make sure the bringer of beer is the worst cook). Another person can bring meats, one can bring salads and desserts and the last person brings neat snacks and cheeses.

The most popular drink at tailgate parties is beer. That doesn't mean that everyone likes it or that beer is the only drink you are allowed to serve, but beer is the favorite in all weather. If you don't have all Martini drinkers or something similar, make sure there is beer at your party. Most people like Bud and Lite or an import or micro-brewery beer like Leinenkugels'. Better stock a non-alcoholic beer too.

If you are required to bring hard liquor for the group but don't know your friends' preferences, consult the chart on page 120. It is safe to bring vodka, gin and maybe a bourbon. Vodka connoisseurs tell me that most vodkas are the same as long as they are charcoal filtered. That means you can buy a high-priced brand and save the bottle for ego refilling, if that is your thing. Gordon's is always a safe gin because it isn't a cheap label and many say it is identical to a more expensive green-bottled brand. Beam is an acceptable bourbon and Jack Daniels is an ideal blend. Both can be found on sale frequently.

The temptation is always there to have your bar stocked with expensive name brands. Since you are entertaining special people (your friends and family), it's OK. The fact that college football tailgates are special occasions to many people is another excuse to get the "good stuff." However, if you tailgate regularly with the same people, we recommend that you get just what you like. Don't try to please (or impress) everyone else.

Jello Shots

J ust west of Illinois' Memorial Stadium, there are endless rows of orange and blue tailgaters and entertainment tents on game day. The parking lot surface is mostly grass, so tailgaters have the opportunity to be creative. They can sink tent poles, build fires and do other things not allowed to people who park in paved lots.

Besides being Illinois' homecoming game, it was also fast approaching Halloween when I was last at Memorial Stadium. So I wasn't surprised when I spotted a pumpkin carved as Fighting Illini. After all, it is the right color! The Illini fans who carved this pumpkin were utilizing a tent made out of blue tarp, bungeed to a dark blue Chrysler mini-van. Under their shelter, they had a serving table surrounded by blue captain's chairs with orange legs. The pre-Halloween cold drizzle sure wasn't going to ruin a tailgating opportunity for these fans.

Approaching with my camera loaded for action, I greeted these tailgaters and explained that their tent interested me. While admiring their engineering, I was handed a small shot glass filled with a blue substance that looked like jello. Paul Gilligan, the tent proprietor and a local realtor said, "Try this jello."

"Why," I asked.

"Drink it, it's cold out!"

Wow! It sure didn't taste like my wife's jello. There was a very strong taste of vodka. My mind ran through the endless possibilities. These could pass inspection by any policeman or stadium usher as they ask, "What's that?"

"Jello." I could bring in enough for a whole group. Enough to last a whole game. I could just imagine hearing, "No thanks, no more jello for me. I'm driving."

The beautiful concoction was the creation of the tailgate hostess Joan Hansen. She said she borrowed the idea from a friend. She made the shots with both blueberry and orange flavored jello for Illinois school colors, but due to the rainbow of flavors and colors available, you could easily match up your team's colors.

Don't worry about the taste. As one of the tailgaters at the Illinois party noted, "They all have the same flavor. Vodka."

To make jello shots, Joan suggest taking your favorite jello color and dissolving it in one cup of boiling water. Then add one cup of vodka. Pour this mixture into disposable shot-sized medicine cups. Chill these cups until serving.

To serve these shots, you'll need toothpicks. Take the lid off the shot. Run the toothpick around the inside of the cup. Put the lid back on and shake the jello down. Then remove the lid and let the jello slide down your throat.

What to Drink

Since frequent tailgaters already know what their regular guests like to drink, this section is to help plan for occasional new guests of which you have no prior knowledge. By using these surveys and tabulations, you can see what the general public likes. It is our hope that the knowledge will make you better prepared and offer you some interesting trivia for tailgate conversation.

I don't know anything about beer, what should I buy?

Beverage World published the following list in November of 1993 of the most popular beers in the United States.

America's Most Popular Types of Beer	
Type Beer	Percent
Premium	35.4
Lights	31.6
Popular	21.7
Imported	4.4
Malt Liquor	4.3
Super Premium	2.5
Other	2

America's Favorite Brands of Beers

Domestic	Million Cases Sold in U.S.	Imported	Million Cases Sold in U.S.
Budweiser	645.9	Heineken	26.7
Miller Lite	243.8	Corona Extra	13.0
Bud Light	185.5	Beck's	9.8
Coor's Light	172.9	Molson Golden	8.5
Busch	133.8	Latts Blue	6.0
Milwaukee's Best	94.0	Amstell Light	5.5

from *Jobson's Liquor Handbook 1993*

I have no idea what kind of liquor or mixers to buy.

Gin, Vodka, Tequilla, Bourbon, Rum.... there are so many choices when you go into the liquor store. And what do you buy to put in drinks with them? Sprite, Coke, Vermouth, Soda Water, the choices seem endless. To help you in your next shopping expedition, *The Louisville Courier Journal* published a survey in February of 1994 showing the favorite cocktails of Americans. The results are in the following chart.

Low/Non-Alcoholic Beer

Type Beer	Thousands Sold
O'Douls	950
Sharps	600
Old Milwaukee NA	300
Coor's Cutter	270
Kingsburry	220
Pabst NA	67
Texas Light	30
Clausthaler	30

From *Beverage Industry* 1-94

America's Favorite Mixed Drinks

Mixed Drink		Percent
Tonic	w/Vodka (52.2%) or Gin (47.8%)	15.7
Martini	w/Vodka (44%) or Gin (56%)	11.0
Bloody Mary		10.2
Rum and Cola		10.2
Margarita		9.2
Screwdriver		9.0
Bourbon and Cola		7.4
7and 7		7.0
Bourbon and Water		6.6
Scotch and Soda		5.6

America's Favorite Brands of Liquor (1993)

Liquor Brand	Thousand Cases Sold
Bacardi Rum	6,170
Smirnoff Vodka	5,752
Seagram's Gin	4,300
Jim Beam Bourbon	3,730
Seagram's Seven Crown	3,700
Popov Vodka	3,560
Jack Daniel's Black	3,555
Bacardi Breezer	3,350
Canadian Mist	3,090
Absolut Vodka	2,950

Reprinted from *Beverage Industry*, April 1994

America's Top Wine Cooler Brands

Brand	Market Share
Bartles & Jaymes	41.2
Seagrams	30.1
Bacardi Breezer	10.2
Jack Daniel's	5.9

Reprinted from *Advertising Age,* for 52 weeks ending 10-2-93

America's Favorite Soft Drinks

Brand	Market Share
Coca-Cola Classic	19.5
Pepsi Cola	15.4
Diet Coke	9.7
Diet Pepsi	5.7
Dr. Pepper	5.5
Mountain Dew	4.6
Sprite	4.1
Seven-Up	2.8

Reprinted from Beverage *World*, March 1994

Talk the Talk

W hat is tailgating? What is a tailgate? *Funk and Wagnall's Standard Encyclopedia Dictionary* gives the following definitions:

tailgate (tāl'gāt') n. a hinged or vertically sliding board or gate closing the back end of a truck, wagon, etc.

tailgating (tāl'gāt'ing) v.t. to drive too close from behind for safety.

The above definitions don't really describe our subject. Tailgate is short for tailgate picnic or tailgate party. Tailgating is short for a phrase using the intransitive verb picnicking as in tailgate picnicking.

We Americans have the habit of shortening phrases or groups of words with the short form becoming a *neologism*, an old word with a new meaning. "Hamburger sandwich" has become simply the hamburger, for example, and most of the time simply "burger."

For your enjoyment, *The Tailgater's Handbook* gives the following, more accurate, definitions for our favorite outdoor sport.

tailgate (tāl'gāt') n. 1. The rear enclosure of a truck, station wagon or van providing either shelter or serving surface for tailgaters. 2. v. To picnic from one's vehicle in the parking lot of a stadium. TAILGATING Picnicking from a vehicle in the stadium parking lot.

tailgater (tāl'gāt'er) n. A person who participates in a tailgate.

Other Terms to Know:

Al.ma Ma.ter (al'me mä'ter) n. 1. A song extolling the virtues of or dedication to a school. 2. A college/ university from which a person has graduated.

Bar (bär) n. 1. a cake or candy prepared in a baking dish, cut into rectangles (bars) and held in a hand while eaten by tailgaters. 2. An establishment serving drinks, esp. alcoholic drinks. 3. -v.t. To put down someone with words or gestures.

Bowl (bōl) n. 1. An ampitheater of stadium housing an annual college football game. 2. A deep round dish from which Chili is served.

Bolt (bolt) n. 1. A rod used to hold something like a roof rocket or tent pole in place with a head on one end and threads on the other. 2. v.i. To move, quickly, suddenly from someone's tailgate. He bolted! 3. v.t. To gulp one's food. Don't bolt your food!

Bun.gee Cord (bun'gee) n. A flexible rubber or elastic cord with a hook on each end used to fasten tarps to vehicles and trailers.

Cool.er (kōo/ler) n. 1. An ice chest used by tailgaters to keep foods and drinks cold. 2. A wine drink made from wine and soda.

Crim.son Tide (crim/sun/tīd) n. 1. Alabama's team name symbolized by an elephant. 2. Bad laundry soap.

Frisbee (friz/bēe) n. Flying saucer type disk sailed between at least two people (or one person and a dog) in a pitch-and-catch parking lot ritual.

Fry (frī) v.t. 1. To cook bratwurst over coals on a grill. 2. n. A social gathering of people eating brats.

Hawk.er (hôk/er) n. One who sells parking spaces, programs or other related goods (never game tickets) and services on game day, from a street or sidewalk location.

Hawk.eye (hôk/i) n. A native or fan of Iowa.

Hoagie (hō/gēe) n. A submarine sandwich common to the Allegheny Mountain states.

Hokies (ho kees) n. Virginia Tech fan or grad.

Hoos.ier (hōoz/her) n. an Indiana fan or resident.

Ivy (ī/vē) n. 1. Formerly powerful eastern football league. 2. A plant which grows on walls of buildings (not edible).

Jeet (jēet) A Pittsburgh sentence asking the question, "Did you eat?" usually answered with, "Notjetjew." (Not yet, did you?)

Pro (pro) n. 1. A professional sport. 2. A professional athlete. 3. A proficient tailgater.

PVC (pēe/vēe/cēe) n. Acronym for Poly Vinyl Chloride. Plastic pipe usually used in tailgate engineering and plumbing.

Road.trip (rōd/trip) n. A visit by a college student or alumnus to a distant campus. – v.i. To take a roadtrip.

Scalp.er (skalp/er) n. entrempreneur who sells tickets from curbside locations near a stadium. They usually buy very cheaply from people with extra tickets and resell them at a profit.

School (skool) n. Any institution that plays college football.

Slather (slàth/er) v.t. 1. To daub thickly with condiments, usually mustard. 2. To spend or use profusely.

Tarp (tarp) n. A low cost sheet of light weight, weatherproof, plastic fabric used to erect expedient tents, wind screens and sun shelters by tailgaters.

Zip (zip) n. a fan of the U. of Akron.

In Closing

Last year no college official threatened to move his team to another city unless the taxpayers bought a new stadium for the team with skyboxes. No college players made any threatening or taunting shoe commercials. Last year there were no college football playoffs, yet college football survives and is more popular than ever.

Each fall, significant numbers of kids enter college. Many of these students eventually attend football games: some for the party, some for the sport, and some just because it's the thing to do. Most of these students, however, graduate and become productive alumni.

Each winter, colleges across America mail football ticket applications to almost three million alumni with a return deadline of June first. Each year over two million people send back these ticket mailers along with large checks. It doesn't matter how bad the teams are, most of the true fans still come. They come because they are part of that college and attending games is part of their own tradition. They come for the party, the game, to see old classmates and some still come because, hey, it's the thing to do.

Each year almost two million alumni tailgate and fry over 12,000,000 brats washed down with 25,000,000 beers. They grill millions of hamburgers, hot dogs and chickens too. They consume mountains of cookies and tons of pasta salad. They will drink pop, tea, beer, coffee and mixed drinks by the tank car load.

These same alumni and fans will buy vehicles suited for tailgating. They will raise flags. They will collect and seek out new gadgets to make their tailgates better and, perhaps, turn a few heads.

They will pass these rituals on to their children, who will in turn pass them on to their children. And so it goes on: tailgating, an American tradition since 1904.

Recommended by the Tailgater's Handbook

During the past four years, we have compared many products for tailgating. The following logos represent the companies who have earned our recommendation. Their logos are each followed by the specific products we recommend and a reference for where to find more information in this book. Try these products, you won't be sorry.

Academy Broadway: The gazebo canopy (page 28) and the folding picnic table (page 34).

Leinenkugel's Beer: Leinenkugel's Red and Original beers (page 58).

Johnsonville: Bratwurst (page 74).

The Fridge: Freezable single drink coolers (page 38).

Igloo: Igloo ice chests and coolers (page 37).

Kingsford: Matchlight charcoal
(page 43).

Campus Collection: Licensed cologne
(page 13)

Char-Broil: Portable gas and charcoal grills (page 43).

Rubbermaid:
Food storage
containers
(page 41).

The South Bend Chocolate Company:
Licensed chocolates (page 110).

The Pasta Shoppe: Licensed
pastas (page 96)

Coleman: the Coleman Kitchen (page 39),
the Coleman Stove (page 43) and the
15000 BTU Bulk Heater (page 61).

The Top 30 Tailgate Schools in America

(Plus a few notable others)

Georgia

Tailgating at Georgia goes back all the way to the 1929 15-0 upset victory over Yale on the day they dedicated Sanford Stadium. Fans of today continue this proud tradition. Some have been known to arrive the day before a game just to set up and party. On game day tailgaters start to arrive around 8:00 in the morning.

Everywhere you look is a sea of red and there are signs everywhere that proclaim, "How 'Bout Them Dogs?", "O'Malley's Tavern" and "Bulldog Club of Savannah" along with many other such notices. Also there is smoke from a thousand grills. It's one big party. When Georgia plays Florida the game is referred to as "The World's Largest Cocktail Party" by ABC as well as others. Drinking at Georgia tailgates is legal, but only if you are 21. It's enforced, too.

One interesting ritual for UGA games is the march of the football team through the fans' parking lots. The players are bused down to the parking lot. They then walk back, in uniform, through the lot to the stadium. The fans line their route and cheer wildly.

Georgia had the highest score among all colleges in *The Tailgater's Handbook*'s rating chart. They just may be number one.

The World's Largest Cocktail Party!

Georgia has everything...

With custom vans and delicious barbecue, school spirit goes hand-in-hand with southern hospitality

Fans are everywhere!

The team even walks through the tailgaters while going to the game

Louisville

Approaching a Cardinal's football game in Louisville (pronounced Louieville by most of the nation and Louavul by the natives) is exciting, to say the least. Their stadium sits at the edge of the State Fairgrounds, south of downtown near the intersection of their two largest freeways. You can get traffic reports for the Cardinal Stadium area on most stations as there can be as many as four helicopters circling the parking lots on game day. When you pull into the lot, the excitement only increases.

Cardinal fans are the best partiers in America. A 360-degree view from any spot in the parking lots would probably show a six-foot tall Cardinal riding a motorcycle, Magilla Gorilla, four or five radio tailgate shows with music blaring, people walking around drinking and socializing, the U of L band and some great tailgate setups. Some of the fans are such great tailgaters that they only visit the games for a minute or two and then get back to their RV for the party.

Not only do these Louisville people tailgate, but they become legends. The Louisville Sports Information office can actually give you the names and locations in the parking lot of some of their more famous tailgaters. This is the only college in America that can do that.

There is a party everywhere at Cardinal Stadium!

...even the sky

Ohio State

The Olentangy River flows southward through farm country on its way to Columbus. Its gentle waters pass the grave of President Rutherford B. Hayes just 20 miles north of the Ohio State campus.

Flowing south, the river is crossed by bridges near downtown, that on game day Saturdays, seem to be designed strictly for walking as the acres of parking on the West Bank release their fans to cross the river to mammoth Ohio Stadium. There are cars for 95,000 people parked on both sides of the river as well as all four sides of the stadium There are open lots, reserved lots, RV lots and multi-storied garages too.

North of the stadium and across the street is a lot packed with motor homes. Everyone seems to know each other and share freely between tail-gates. There are grills everywhere and a high-stakes poker game. However, the lot is perhaps most famous for a rather elaborate joke that one of the lot's "regulars" plays on lot newcomers. The regular is parked near what appears to be a utility pole cemented into the parking lot. It has all the hook-ups for water, sewer and power. He even offers to help his neighbor set up, and pulls out equipment to tap into the lines. People gather and ask him how he was lucky enough to get a spot with a utility hookup. After the game, when people are enjoying the postgame tailgate, this trickster un-hooks all the lines from the pole and then picks up the pole itself, tucks it under his arm and takes it into the RV. It has been said that people actually go over to the spot and rake their foot over the pavement to see what happened.

Ohio Stadium hosts 95,000 fans and almost as many tailgaters on both sides of the river

"Tailgreat" at Illinois

Back in 1986 the University of Illinois athletic promotions department decided to spice up their fan excitement with a contest among tailgaters. The contest was to be called "Tailgreat" and feature numerous prizes judged by campus personalities like the radio color voice of the Illini football network.

The first year of Tailgreat drew over 20,000 people. The atmosphere was similar to that of a carnival midway with plenty of food and fun. There was a dunking booth dropping a Bo Schembeckler look-alike into the water. There was a dance review with orange t-shirted alumni performing to and "singing" the music of the Beach Boys, with a small change from "Help Me Rhonda" to "Go Illini." A full-ringed heavyweight wrestling show was staged with an Illini chief look-alike entering the ring to dispatch the bad guys. A gorilla played a saxophone. The Oscar Mayer weinermobile was there as well as a 20-foot high "Rube Goldberg" contraption with a Teddy Bear hitting a Cardinal which triggered a mechanism to dispense beer out of a tap below.

Tailgreat has grown, evolved and changed over the years. It was continued without rule changes for seven years. Now it has become more of a cook-off or food contest. Amateurs and professionals compete for cash and prizes. The winning recipes are published each year in a fund-raising cookbook.

Illinois is a great tailgate school

They have something for everyone...

There are plenty of elaborate setups & custom vans

The band does it up in style for "Tailgreat"

And there is plenty of room for vehicles of all types

Penn State's Student Section

Forget what you have heard about the student sections at Notre Dame, Nebraska, Tennessee, Army or Wisconsin. There is one student section that stands above all others for noise, spirit and tradition. They sit in the southeastern corner of Beaver Stadium and root for their Nittany Lions.

Penn State students buy almost 20,000 football season tickets, more than any other group of undergrads in America. They also make more noise than any other students. After warm-ups, but before the teams come back out for the game, rookie fans get their first taste of the students. They belt out the words, "We Are..." The rest of the stadium returns with "Penn State." Followed by another "We Are," and again "Penn State" from the softer 73,000 old folks. The students are so loud that people across the field can feel it. It's great! It goes on for minutes til, I'm sure, some people pass out from hyperventilation.

Then as the Nittany Lion mascot brings the team out of the south end zone tunnel the student body lets out, in unison, a lion's roar. It is awesome. Loud, fun, intimidating and completely college football. The band joins into the general hullabaloo in their old fashioned uniforms by playing a chorus of "Hail to the Lions" and the place goes wild.

Beaver Stadium has the loudest student section in America!

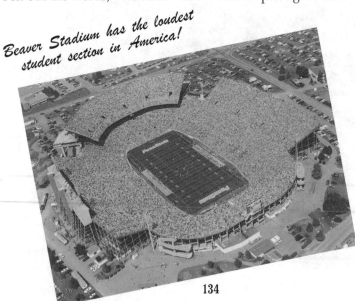

Michigan

Michigan fans don't have the luxury of great big lots in which to tailgate. Their parking is wedged between buildings, practice fields, patches of trees and fairways of the golf course. People, being separated by natural or man-made barriers into little enclaves, seem to become more neighborly than fans in a thousand-car lot. It seems more intimate and less threatening to be in a small area.

Everywhere you look are huge flags all blue with the block maize M. You can hear "Hail to the Victors" from tape players in every lot or from cars driving by searching for their entrance or a vacancy.

The menu is normal for Midwestern tailgaters. There's chili, burgers, brats, plenty of beer, mixed drinks, pop and corn chips. The chips at a blue-blooded Michigan tailgate, however, have to be maize and blue. That's right, if there is a way to serve blue and gold food, the Michigan fans will do it.

Just before the game, the Michigan band marches through the parking area to the stadium. Fans get pumped up with the sound of the drums and cymbals and the cheers of "Go Blue!" The tailgaters generally use the band's approach as notice to pack up and follow the crowd into Michigan Stadium.

The largest crowds in football tailgate here

Notre Dame

There is still a place where you can go to experience the feelings and sights that made college football great: the University of Notre Dame.

Approaching Notre Dame from almost every direction, the first glimpse of campus is the beautiful golden dome of the Administration building. This building is the stage for one of the most well-attended repeating concerts in collegiate America. No, not the Grateful Dead. We're talking about the Grateful Living, also known as the Fighting Irish Marching Band. About two hours before each home game, people start to gather in front of the Administration building's steps to get a good view for the concert. By the time the band arrives, there are 20,000 people standing on lawns, sitting on shoulders, hanging from trees and sitting on roofs. The band always marches from this concert to the stadium along the same route, just in time for its pregame show. The march is as well attended as the concert, with the people straining to see the Irish Guard in their kilts as well as the Leprechaun and band marchers. The strains of the Notre Dame Victory March brings many tears as well as cheers as the band cranks up.

Notre Dame capitalizes on its national prominence and no longer has a season ticket program for alumni. (However, about 5,000 seats were grandfathered under the old program.) All students get tickets first and then people wanting Irish tickets get put into a lottery. The lottery winners only get one or two (at most) sets of tickets per year. That means there are 40,000 new faces at every game.

The best tailgating takes place in the Red West and other lots close to the stadium. The same people come week after week and have repeated their routines long enough to become quite proficient. Other areas, farther away from the stadium, actually have people that come to every game without tickets. If they can't beg or buy a ticket from a passerby, they can always watch the game on a portable TV while they tailgate.

The pregame band concert

136

A young Irish fan finds the best seat in the house

The campus is packed early every game day for the band's march to the stadium

Navy, America's oldest college band, serenades the Irish fans

Nebraska

Is it good teams that produce loyal fans, or loyal fans that cause good teams? Whichever it is, Nebraska has great football teams and even better fans. Riding back-to-back national championship teams, Nebraska will surely sell out next season's games as they have sold out every game in Lincoln since 1962. Nebraska's Memorial Stadium holds over 75,000 people, most of which come from the Eastern Nebraska, Omaha, Lincoln area. Then there are the "out-staters" (rest of Nebraska residents) who drive from far away towns like Scottsbluff or Chardon, some more than 400 miles from Lincoln. Then there are the out-of-state fans from far, far away.

Ike Maggert hasn't been a student at Nebraska since 1960, but he and his wife, Rita, still go to every (home and away) game, which is quite a feat, considering they live in Atlanta, Georgia. Ike, a realtor says that there are other Atlanta Cornhuskers too. There's the Collingsworths who make about 97% of the Nebraska games. They all meet on Thursday night for ESPN's football kickoff show. Friday is their travel day. The only time they travel on Saturday is when Ike has a closing or big sale pending. Then they fly to Kansas City by 9:00 am, rent a car and drive to Lincoln (3$\frac{1}{2}$ hours) only stopping at a deli or KFC to stock-up for their tailgating.

For road games Ike has a banner for the motel/hotel balcony and another for the stadium. If the locals won't let them put the banner up, they just carry it around the stadium evoking cheers from Cornhuskers and lesser greetings from opposing fans.

Nebraska tailgaters park near the stadium and move around in their lots for socializing and food tasting

LSU

L ate on Thursday people start to arrive in RVs for Saturday's game at LSU. The Tiger fans, mostly from instate, like to get a good spot and raise their purple flags. They also need a restful Friday because they always have an all-day tailgate party on Saturday. Almost all LSU games are at night allowing the fans more time to be creative with their menus and setups.

The backbone of an LSU tailgate is Cajun/Arcadian food. The parking lots will have crawfish boils, people serving jambalaya and shrimp. They prepare blackened chicken or fish sandwiches too, all which need some very cold beer to settle properly. Of course, there are burgers, brats and dogs too, but the character and smells of an LSU tailgate is different from any other in America.

On the edge of tailgating lots is a hill with a road called North Stadium Drive. Fans love to congregate there because two hours before the game the LSU football team, wearing sweats and game faces, walks down that hill into Tiger Stadium .Then about a half hour before the game the band marches down the hill after a rendition of the fight song.

Night games are the rule at LSU, but tailgating is even better in the cooler air

Clemson's Tiger Tailgate Show

In 1976 while voters were preparing for a national election, Jerry Arp, a 1972 Clemson grad, was kicking off the nation's first radio network tailgate show. Jerry's idea was to create an atmosphere where the fans would get more psyched up for games. He started with just a handful of stations and a lot of enthusiasm. The idea took off and has grow to include more than 35 stations and gained the full support of the University community.

The show is performed in the parking lot adjacent to the Stadium. There is a large stage from which a radio host conducts the events. The cheerleaders make an appearance in front of the stage to pep up the assembled spectators. The band comes by and plays the fight song, and there are interviews with dignitaries. They predict the outcome of the game and give traffic, weather and other relevant tailgating reports.

Every 15 minutes there is a remote report from Tiger basketball coach Rick Barnes who rides through tailgating areas in a golf cart that is known as the "Paw Patrol." Barnes, accompanied by a driver from the Clemson Sports Network, finds fans and alumni and persuades them to come on the air and talk about the weather, the game, their recipes and other facets of that day's outing.

The Tiger Tailgate Show has a little bit of everything

The Paw Patrol circles the lot at every home game

The atmosphere is similar to a pep rally

The interviews always make for wacky fun

Indiana

In 1960 Indiana moved their football games from their old Memorial Stadium, wedged between the buildings of campus on Tenth Street, to their new Memorial Stadium on 17th Street. The old stadium had room for only 30,000 people, counting temporary bleachers, while the new model has over 50,000 seats that all faced the center of the field. The real benefit, however, of the new stadium site was that there was virtually unlimited space for parking, field houses, practice fields and more.

At the stadium, tailgaters set up about three hours before game kickoff. There are grass, gravel and paved lots. The grass areas, the farthest from the stadium, host the professional tailgaters. These people have huge cookers, big picnic tables, tall flags and room to spread out. The paved lots, by contrast, are for the big-givers. They have small reserved spaces. These tailgaters don't have the room to do much cooking, but they are so close to the stadium that they can come out at half time to enjoy a drink and a sandwich. These reserved lot folks tend to just pop a tailgate or a trunk, fix a cold sandwich or open a bucket of chicken and then go into the stadium. The people further out spend more time in effort in creating the perfect tailgating ambiance.

If you don't like the color red, avoid Indiana games, because the stadium and parking lots are bathed in it. There are flags everywhere you look and the people have everything from sweaters and socks to cars and vans in the Hoosier red.

Memorial Stadium has enough tailgating space for everybody

Purdue's Annual Tailgating Contest

The Boilermaker Backers, Purdue's booster club, desiring to promote fan interest, held a tailgate party contest before a Purdue vs. Illinois game. The first year (1993) there were prizes like a trip for eight to Switzerland, transportation and hotel included. Since then they have added prizes and even changed the contest to allow winners at different levels.

The Boiler Backers put out a brochure to tailgaters in their season ticket mailer. It shows photos of past entrants and explains the rules and prizes. In 1995, they added to the fun with a cook-off. Professional barbecuers came and competed for big cash prizes.

On the 20th anniversary of Purdue grad Neil Armstrong's moon walk, Purdue University set up a special event called "The Cosmic Cafe." It featured a party of famous Purdue alums meeting at the moon. Depicted in the photo are Neil Armstrong, Purdue Pete, Orville Redenbacker, Amelia Earhart, Bob Griese and Marilyn Quayle. In the background is a NASA space capsule and the North end of Ross Aide Stadium.

Purdue "celebrities" congregate at the Cosmic Cafe

"Rail"gating at South Carolina

Fans are used to seeing college football stadium parking lots full of tailgaters with vans and motor homes. Some tailgaters set up so elaborately that you think they are never going to leave. But take a trip to Columbia, South Carolina and you'll see something that will blow your mind. A real tailgater's railroad.

Columbia developer, Ed Robinson, was bothered by a CSX Southern rail spur which, though abandoned, still ran right next to Williams-Brice Stadium. The rail spur took up space, looked bad and was a hazard to drivers. Robinson decided to do something about it. He saved 22 cabooses that were headed for the scrap yard and offered them to alumni at $45,000 apiece unfinished. Thus began the Cockaboose Railroad.

These cabooses are not just shelter, they have been sold to individuals and corporations and finished off in style. They have posh living rooms, upper decks, rest rooms, bars, kitchens, gas grills and even cable TV. Many are even wired with closed-circuit TV which shows USC road games for the fans who can't make the trip.

Since the Cockaboose railroad, Ed has developed a golf course for the USC golf team. The course was designed by P.B. Dye and has 27 holes. On the practice range sits a Cockaboose with a platform on top for the golf coach to view shots by his team. Ed has also developed the Tailgate Park facility for Gamecock fans. This is a special area for tailgaters near the Cockabooses. Ed is now working on college developments in other states.

A view from the stadium shows tailgaters in lots, cockabooses and Tailgate Park

Along the tracks at the Cockaboose RR

Ed Robinson and his Cockaboose

Before

After... What a Difference!

Florida

What tailgating space there is near Ben Hill Griffin Stadium at Florida Field is snapped up early by orange and blue clad Gator fans. Tailgating is done in a variety of lots around the track, baseball, basketball and football fields, micro-lots wedged around buildings and whatever else they can find. Many people just opt for the numerous college town bars/sandwich houses that line the campus.

A Florida home game is one of the most enjoyable tradition-filled, hands-on audience participation events in America. The "Pride of the Sunshine State," the Fightin' Gator Marching Band rocks the house all day long. Mr. Two-Bits, George Edmonson, a Tampa resident, comes to every game to lead each section in the "Two-bits, four-bits" cheer. Then at the end of the third quarter the band always strikes up "We are the Boys From Old Florida." The fans link arms and sway left and right to the music.

Homecoming at most colleges is when the alumni really try harder to get back for the game, usually the only one most of them get to each year. At Florida, 83,000 tickets are sold for each game because for Florida's graduates, every week is homecoming. If you don't buy a season ticket, you'll struggle to find a seat for the homecoming game. More than 65 years ago, Florida started holding a pep rally the night before he homecoming game called the "Gator Growl." This event has evolved into the largest student-run pep rally in America. They annually pack in 70,000 fans for an evening of entertainment and school spirit.

The lack of parking doesn't dampen the fun at Gainesville

Auburn "Tiger Walk"

Auburn fans arrive early and stay late. They tailgate on the road sides as well as on the intramural fields. The big ritual at an Auburn home game is to fire the grill and relax with good food and friends.

The Tiger (or is it War Eagles?) football team, for many seasons, has taken the "Tiger Walk" to home games. The players leave their athletic dorm wearing jackets, ties and game faces. They walk right through the sea of orange and blue fans en route to Jordan-Hare Stadium. The past few seasons, however, Auburn fans have also taken this event on the road surrounding the Tigers' bus and giving the team a cheering human sea to part on their way into their competitor's stadium.

The Auburn band stages a pregame concert/warm-up on a practice field near the stadium. Fans listen to renditions of the day's stadium music shows. The band forms into marching order and then takes their show right through the fans en route to the stadium. War Eagle fans cheer, clap and swell with pride as this first class college band heralds another Fall Saturday.

The Tiger Walk

The band's walk

Colorado

Colorado fans are lucky. They have a great Buffalo football team, one of the world's prettiest views and an administration at the school that loves tailgating.

Big givers are allowed to park in the reserved Gold Lot, just east of Folsum Field. This parking is special because it's done on grass allowing the partiers a soft carpet and a place to create. Everyone seems to have a grill going by late morning. There are some with small table top grills and others with the larger varieties. A group of ten Denver residents make the trip to Boulder towing their special cooker. This portable kitchen has buffalo horns, a CU logo, a huge smoke stack and a refrigerated tap line for beer. They usually entertain with sides of meat, tons of ribs, or whatever else sounds good.

Looking south at Folsum Field

Maryland

Probably the most unique thing about Maryland's tailgating is its sheer size. Parking lot one, adjacent to the "bottom of the horseshoe" of Byrd Stadium is renowned for being HUGE and filled to capacity. The sea of red, white, gold and black seems to go on forever.

Terrapin faithful can be spotted grilling the usual favorites: hot dogs, chicken and hamburgers prepared on the hibachi. Tailgaters bring card tables, lawn chairs, flags, coolers full of cold ones and the other necessities hours before game time. Some RVs actually camp out the day before to ensure that they will have a prime spot on game day. The theme for every game is "Kick back and Wear Red."

Maryland tailgaters also come out in force for Lacrosse. Maybe that's just another excuse for Terp fans to tailgate.

Byrd stadium is surrounded at every home game by tailgaters

Maryland fans "pump-up" hours before the game

Oregon

Official tailgating at Oregon starts about four hours before the game when the lots open. Unofficial tailgating starts a little earlier for the folks who already have set up in the street, in line, waiting for the gates to open. Duck fans want to get there early because they are excited about their football program. Oregon has risen to the heights, and Washington doesn't come in and push them around anymore.

Weather is generally very mild for Duck games with the coldest day of the 1995 season being only mid- to high-40s. To capitalize on good weather and renewed spirit, the Alumni Association has a huge tent at every game that serves up to 3000 people. They call it the "world's largest tailgate" as there are tables and chairs, a food court, memorabilia shops, bars, and even big screen TVs. If you don't want to go to the trouble of preparing everything for a tailgate you just go to the tent.

On game day tailgaters set up on gravel lots that surround Antzen Stadium. They hoist green flags with yellow block "O" emblems or mean-looking cartoon ducks. They cook the usual burgers and dogs, but there is one native food, the homegrown Salmon Burger. Oregon fans will be the first to tell you, "you don't eat raw fish." You cook salmon burgers like a hamburger. The only difference is that it's great change of pace and it's better for you.

Duck decorations are the thing at Oregon games

Helmets, tents and even lawn chairs have to be in green and yellow if you are tailgating at Oregon.

quack, quack!

Northwestern

The biggest problem with the rise of Northwestern football fortunes is that the best tailgating lots are now reserved for big givers. Prior to having winning seasons, NU fans could drive up to the lots west of Dyche Stadium and, after paying five bucks, take a good parking spot that would have afternoon shade. There were some fine tailgate parties in that lot. Now the big givers park there. They get out of their cars and proceed into the stadium where they are entertained by the university.

Probably destined for the grave, however, is the north end zone "cafe" at Wildcat games. This was a large tent with tables and chairs, kind of like a picnic area at Comisky Park. The clientele were the most loyal alumni and people the school wanted to entertain. Now, just like in the 50s and 60s, Northwestern tickets are scarce. Look for the return of a bleacher section in that area, replacing the tent, and increasing the seating capacity in the stadium.

Northwestern tailgaters generally gather East of Dyche Stadium. The most unusual part about Northwestern, however, is the fact that thousands of their students actually tailgate. They car pool to the east lot, set up tables, chairs, speakers, coolers and grills. They cook chicken, burgers, brats, wings and consume kegs of beer. Prior to mid-1995 most of these students stayed in the parking lot too! Even during the game! They usually only visited the games. The reason was that once you leave the stadium at Northwestern, you can't get back in. They have no pass-outs for tailgaters to go out to the parking lot at halftime. Consequently students used to the old Northwestern tradition of losing and partying in the parking lot, had to now get used to winning and staying in their seats for the whole game.

The average SAT for applying Northwestern freshmen is 1240 — can't you tell?

The Kappa Sig
Keg Stand
Team

Fraternities and
Sororities set up huge
gatherings east of the
stadium

Early arrivals
west of the
stadium

Iowa State

If you drive about a half hour north from Des Moines on I-35, you'll come to Ames and Iowa State. Here the Cyclones play football in one of those double-decked stadiums like Kentucky and West Virginia have. All the seats generally face toward the center of the field; there are two decks so more people can get close to the field, and they are far enough from the busy center of campus that they can have great parking and room to build basketball arenas, among other things.

Iowa State has one of the finest tailgating parking lots in America. The stadium sits on the Eastern edge of things with the basketball arena on the West. In between is about a mile of paved parking. This parking is varied too. There are open areas and there are little courts with curbed off areas of grass, trees and shrubs. The ambiance is definitely classy.

To go with these nice surroundings, Iowa State fans will surprise you with their culinary efforts. Bill Doubler, for example, likes to use a wok to cook oriental foods for his family. These Jefferson, Iowa natives serve dishes like Chinese chicken wings, egg rolls and fried rice that smell and look great!

Cyclone fans, mostly sporting yellow and red car flags, are everywhere on game day. You can stand at the ISU exit from I-35 and watch these fans feed in from all directions like armies. They start arriving very early with the tailgaters really cooking around 11:00. There are a lot of footballs in the air too. They tell me that this is the best way to work off a few brats before game time.

Acres and acres of tailgating are available at Iowa State

The Grove Tradition Ole Miss

The Grove at Ole Miss is a ten-acre plot of ground, heavily shaded by Oaks, near the center of campus and Vaught-Hemingway Stadium. Mississippi fans park around the Grove and set their tailgates up on the lawn under the oaks. It is a beautiful and romantic setting; one that would have served well as a setting for a novel by William Faulkner, who loved Ole Miss and did a great deal of his best work there.

In 1985 Ole Miss coach Billy Brewer began a tradition of taking his football team, two hours before game time, down the sidewalk which runs through The Grove en route to the stadium. During this promenade, Ole Miss fans fight for position on either side of the sidewalk and cheer wildly for their team before returning to their tailgates. This recent tradition has continued through the regimes of two more head coaches at Mississippi.

The team walks through the Grove to the stadium every home game - Saturday

Fresh flowers, a drink and good friends make the Grove even better

Wyoming's Tailgate Park

To understand the popularity of tailgating at Wyoming, you must first look at the state's geography. The UW campus is at Laramie in the extreme southeastern corner of the state. Being the only four-year institution in the state, people drive an average of two and a half hours to games and many drive as far as seven hours from Jackson or Cody in the northwestern corner of Wyoming. When people drive that far to a game they want to be reunited with old friends in Tailgate Park.

"It really captures the essence of Wyoming and it's people," said Mark Pajak, the UW Promotions Director. "It's a chance for our fans to get together and see friends and old classmates from all over the state. It's a social event for alumni and even first time visitors to mix."

Tailgate Park is located less than 200 yards from the north entrance to Wyoming's War Memorial Stadium, encompassing more than a square block, it hosts upwards of 5000 fans for all six games each season . There is a theme in the park for each week's tailgating activities centered around Wyoming Cowboy heritage. These activities have included barbecues, chili cook-offs, and staged wild west gun fights.

Historically there is a train ride from campus to a nearby cattle ranch the night before the first game. Then barbecue and dancing under the stars. Then on game day, the ranch hosts an antique car show, five K run, live music and more.

In 1993 *The Sporting News* voted Tailgate Park the top pregame party in the Rocky Mountains.

Cowboy Fans take the train to the ranch party the night before the game (left) and then meet again at Tailgate Park (above)

Army

Tailgaiting is extremely popular at Army. Fans begin to arrive at 7:00 a.m. for a 1:00 p.m. game. Many times they stay on after the game until it is dark. In the 1970s *The Sporting News* rated Army as the best tailgate in America. They still do it right today with both fans who have Rolls Royces and vintage wine or fans who munch beer and brats from the back of a truck.

The march of the Corps of Cadets into Miche Stadium is something every football fan should see. Fans will also love the view of the fall trees along the Hudson River.

Even the Army travels in style to tailgate — yes, that is caviar and a Rolls Royce!

The march of the Corps of Cadets into Miche Stadium

East Carolina

Pirate fans at East Carolina begin coming five hours before their afternoon football games. The loyal alumni who donate enough to the sports program get numbered reserved spaces on well-kept grass lots. That's where their fun begins.

"Ain't it great to tailgate" is the theme the University gave these rabid fans. Everyone is dressed in purple, grills are fired up and people decorate with flair. One group always brings a dance floor and music. One has a vehicle which converts into a pirate ship. This ship raises a real mast with a crow's nest holding a Pirate. Purple window flags are everywhere.

The food of choice in eastern North Carolina is pork barbecue. The region has evolved its own vinegar based barbecue sauce which has become the topping for game day fans as well as their huge off-season tailgating event, "The Great Pirate Purple and Gold Pigskin Pig-Out Party." This hog roast is one more great tailgate in conjunction with the Spring inter-squad game. If you don't count the Indianapolis 500, this event is probably the best springtime tailgate event in America.

Pirate fans have numbered spaces on the grass

Tailgaters believe in eating well at East Carolina — Doesn't the food look great?

N.C. State

Carter-Finley Stadium is located off the North Carolina State campus near the state fairgrounds. Its parking lot is very large, probably several hundred acres surrounded and partitioned by woods. This makes for a great tailgating setting.

Wolfpack fans tend to cluster in groups and have real tailgate parties. Some have weekly themes with particular menus and setups. For example, one group had an Italian restaurant setting with red and white checkered tablecloths and candles. Many people like to roam the parking lot too. They travel, in the vicinity of their vehicle, from one group to the next.

The pregame show or school songs can be heard everywhere in the lot. Because the lot is so large, people who want to boogie down with their own music have their own area. Kids have room to toss frisbees and footballs also.

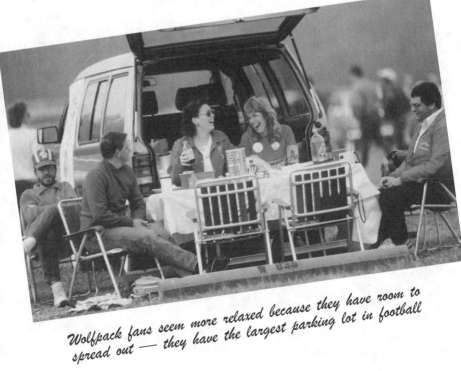

Wolfpack fans seem more relaxed because they have room to spread out — they have the largest parking lot in football

Air Force Academy

One of the biggest treats of an Air Force Saturday in Colorado Springs is to see the Cadet Wing march into Falcon Stadium prior to kickoff. A relatively new school, Air Force, founded in the 1950s has continually added to their stadium so that it now holds over 50,000 fans.

Since almost every game starts at noon, tailgating at Air Force is a constant brunch. Fans start to arrive before 8:00 a.m. and set up grills and stoves to warm and even prepare breakfasts. You'll find a lot of breakfast casseroles, quiche, and precooked dishes because of their great taste and easy preparation on game day. There are also tailgaters actually scrambling eggs and frying bacon. However, there are a few "cheeseheads" from Wisconsin there cooking brats and drinking beer at nine or ten in the morning.

The press is very fond of Air Force too. That's because they are one of the few colleges that serve beer after the game in the press box.

The sight of the entrance of the Cadet Wing is one reason for tailgaters to pack up a little early at Air Force games

Texas Tech

Tailgaters at Texas Tech got a real deal in 1994 when the Raider's athletic staff created Raider Alley. It was the first organized university effort to accommodate tailgaters. Located between the baseball park and the football stadium, this small reserved parking/tailgating facility has doubled in size yearly. The "Alley" now sports stages for live entertainment and room for several hundred cars. All this to make sure Red Raider fans (who donate enough) make a day of it.

Since Raider Alley space is limited, the rest of Tech's 50,000 plus fans gather near the stadium. There are red and black clad fans everywhere. Some fans arrive as much as six hours before on day game (that's 7 a.m.). Being from Texas, of course they cook elaborate barbecues with hot chili during the colder weather.

In Memoriam

The official mascot of Texas Tech University, "Double T," died instantly after colliding with a ramp wall during the Red Raider football game with New Mexico in 1995. The black horse's saddle apparently broke under "Masked Rider" Amy Smart, a junior from Dallas. Smart fell to the stadium turf and the horse charged into a field level exit ramp. University Veterinarian, Dr. Mark Hellman said that the horse died instantly from a blow to the head from colliding with the ramp wall.

"The entire Texas Tech family is saddened by this very tragic event," said Athletic Director Bob Bockrath. "Because of the proud tradition of the Masked Rider at Texas Tech University, this is a stunning blow to all Red Raiders."

The last Tech mascot to die during its tenure was "Happy VI" who succumbed to colic during the night in 1978.

The smell of barbecue fills the air every game day at Tech

Lake Washington

Husky Stadium, built in 1928, sits on the banks of Lake Washington, separated from Puget Sound and the Pacific by a narrow strip of land, a few freeways and a couple of million people. By 1930 people from nearby Seattle began to run their boats up to the stadium and land in the marshes. They would then make a wet hike through the cattails to the game.

By the 1960s, the stadium waterfront was developed and docks were constructed to facilitate Husky fans. Today the area is called "The Waterfront Activity Center" and is available for much more than aquatic football parking. The athletic department administers to the moorings and claims that around 5000 people attend the games via the waterways. There are 238 boat docking slips available that are reserved as many as ten years in advance. A larger number of boaters anchor further out in the lake and are picked up and dropped off by a dozen tour boats before and after the games.

Washington fans are not what you'd call fair-weather tailgaters either. They still come when there is a snow storm and can be seen chipping ice from their ropes and shoveling the docks. However, most Washington games are in beautiful weather next to a beautiful lake. The tailgating is the same as at hundreds of other campuses, only prettier.

Lake Washington allows alternate transportation for Husky fans

Rice

There are plenty of places to tailgate around the 70,000 seat, 46-year old Rice Stadium. That's because it's relatively young as big time college stadiums go. In 1949 Rice won the SWC and the Cotton Bowl ending with a 10-1 record. The city fathers of Houston thought that Rice's old 37,000 seat stadium was not a proper venue for the SWC champions, much less a city with so bright a future. Breaking ground in February and working three shifts a day for nine months, the stadium was ready for the 1950 season.

Rice Stadium was build with room for parking, because in 1950 Houston saw the automobile boom coming. Most other college stadia had been locked-in by their campuses by 1950. Along with big parking lots, Rice has green belts around the stadium with trees and lawns just made for tailgating.

A Rice tradition is for fans to arrive early, find a great shady spot and set chairs, tables, coolers and grills out. Everywhere you look there are laid-back Rice fans in blue and gray.

When it's time for the game, another tradition is lead by the band as they invite the fans down onto the field to help bring out (welcome) the football team. Rice is the smallest Division 1 school in America with only just over 2500 students. The bonding of the fans, alumni and students is much closer than at those huge gatherings at Austin with 36,000 Texas undergraduates.

There's plenty of room to tailgate at Rice!

163

Wake Forest

Demon Deacon fans arrive on game day as much as four hours before kickoff. The setting for their tailgating parties is Western North Carolina in the beautiful Piedmont. You can see Pilot Mountain from the tree-lined parking areas.

Wake Forest gives a free tent and meals for groups of 200 or more so there are many large outings for games. These groups use a special lot as well. Other tailgaters have choices not available to cramped city campus settings. There are parking areas on grass amidst fall foliage. There are also huge green areas right next to Groves Stadium. Here people picnic on the grass with pizza purchased at a tent or the locally famous fried chicken.

The games are often at night so tailgaters at Wake Forest have a relaxed time socializing before all games.

Wake has beautiful scenery...

...and plenty of grassy lawns for picnicking

Georgia Tech

ordered on its southeast side by the high rise buildings of Atlanta, Tech is probably only a couple of miles from the center of town. This fact and the resulting high value of real estate makes parking around Bobby Dodd Stadium/Grant Field pretty valuable. Tech doesn't have huge fields that can be laid out for parking like many colleges. Here money talks! Only the most financially loyal alumni get the prime parking spots.

Other tailgaters rely on fraternity lots, campus building lots and private parking, sometimes in front yards. This doesn't, however, even slightly dampen the spirit of these devoted tailgaters. There are "Yellow Jacket" fans buzzing around all over the campus. The fans' favorite drink seems to be cold beer and the game day tune of preference is "The Ramblin' Wreck," which is piped from speakers in almost every window and from every car.

Wedged into the city, Georgia Tech tailgaters have to squeeze in between buildings

arking is at a premium for Hawkeye fans going to Kinnick Stadium. There are a few "official lots," but most people have to fend for themselves.

Fans approaching the stadium are bombarded with parking lot hawkers (not to be confused with Hawkeyes) yelling, "Park here." They advertise prices of three dollars at the lots more than a mile out and increase their demands to at least seven dollars for right across the street from the stadium. These hawkers aren't hardened like those at a Cubs game. They are boy scouts, ministers, mothers and other volunteers for numerous organizations fortunate enough to have premium parking space. There is even parking at the lot for a country club.

Iowa fans cook the usual tailgate foods like brats, hamburgers, chili and chicken. On a day with "heavy air," there is blue brat smoke hanging in the trees. In addition to being great cooks, Iowa people are probably the nicest football fans you are likely to find. They share their food, rib the opposition fans, eat crow when they lose and make you glad you went to the game.

Exceptionally nice people and small lots make Iowa tailgating unique

Wisconsin

The University of Wisconsin sits right in the middle of a big city (Madison, population 195,000) with much more bustle and confusion than colleges in even larger areas like Boston College, Pitt or even UCLA. Streets, with too much traffic, cross everywhere.

Camp Randall Stadium is located right in an old Midwestern residential area. The surrounding houses are 75 year-old two and three story brick and frame affairs with huge trees and small drives. It's difficult to find tailgating parking except on the few big giver lots east of the stadium between the adjacent university buildings. Most people tailgate in smaller parking lots and yards.

A typical tailgating session occurs every home Saturday at the Madison Clinic, seven blocks (.7 miles) west at Regent and Brooks streets. Here a hundred or so cars use the clinic lot and bathrooms. They set up grills, flag poles, coolers and other traditional items as they surf the lot to taste and talk. Across the street (918 Regent) there is an old three story house converted into an apartment building. The building's porch roof, now with a homemade balcony, has just enough room and strength for the Wisconsin band to crowd in a few thousand pounds of drummers, trombonists, trumpeters and other wild musicians to play "On Wisconsin" and the "Bud" song.

Once you find it, Wisconsin tailgating is as good as any

Michigan State

Spartan Stadium sits in East Lansing, which is separated from the Michigan state capital, Lansing, only by an interstate beltway called I-469. On game days, vehicles migrate to Michigan State from all directions, entering town on any of six separate freeway corridors. It is remarkable to sit on an overpass and count the thousands of little green car flags with the block "S" as State fans pass below. MSU may have more of these car flags on the road than any other college in America.

At the game itself, the small lots close to the stadium are taken by the motor home and big-giver folks. The IM fields, however, provide a great open spot for tailgating. These fields are spacious and grassy, which allows Michigan State fans to spread out and be a little creative with their tailgating. You'll see personal gazebos, grills and even fires on cold days.

Fans start arriving as early as five hours before kickoff and often stay late as well. They set up grills to cook brats and bars to mix Bloody Marys. Everywhere you look are tall flag poles with green flags emblazoned with a big white "S." The youngsters start football tossing and frisbees early and their games are occasionally visited by the older folks who only want to burn off calories, of course.

The MSU players and coaches, after a night at the campus hotel, do their "walk to the stadium" past parents and fans, just as they have since the Duffy Daugherty years. The band also marches to the stadium from their pregame concert down the street. Tailgaters usually leave their vehicles to cheer on the band as it marches by and plays one last rendition of the State fight song. After the last tuba player goes by, it is time to pack up the tailgate and move on to the game.

Tailgating is an art form at Michigan State

Tennessee's Volunteer Navy

The Tennessee River bends slowly westward through Knoxville and passes just south of huge Neyland Stadium. A picture of serenity, its waters have passed through history with Cherokee Indians, explorers like Couture and Chartier, the Civil War and the TVA. Now its meanderings meet with the Tennessee campus and Volunteer football.

The Tennessee campus is a combination of hills, narrow winding streets and limited parking. It is difficult enough to just drive and park, much less tailgate at UT games. So on football Saturdays the river boils with hundreds of vessels, ranging from canoe size to 250,000 ton cruisers. These watercrafts, decorated with orange paint and accents, make up what is known as the "Volunteer Navy." These boats form one of the nation's premier aquatic tailgate parties.

"Where else can you find people this crazy about football?" beams George Mooney, the founder of this navy. Mooney got things started in 1962, just after another expansion of the football stadium. He became more and more frustrated by the traffic mess, until one week he just sailed his boat from his home on the river down to the vicinity of the stadium and tied it to a tree. The idea spread like wildfire and by 1972 more than 2000 people were coming to games by boat.

Today there are docks with spaces for 200 boats for the Vol Navy and even a tunnel under the road so that the fans can get into the stadium safely.

The Volunteer Navy tailgates on the Tennessee River

Northern Illinois

The Huskies of Northern Illinois are at it again, going from the Great West Conference to Independent status and then back to the MAC. Their program is on the move and they want to start playing a few teams closer to home. They didn't get a lot of fans that drove from Dekalb, Illinois to California or Nevada. It also makes sense to change leagues because they (the athletic promotions staff) have really made an effort to have big time tailgating.

Every Husky game sports at least 30 red and white striped corporate/group tents right behind the stadium. Northern fans always have a choice to either prepare their own tailgate or join one of the groups with a tent.

The native foods of Northern Illinois tailgates are the Ribeye Sandwich and the Butterfly Pork Chop Sandwich. If you run out or don't want to bother with packing your own main course, you can always buy one of these specialities from one of the tents.

Tents are a big thing at Northern Illinois, but so are Ribeye Sandwiches!

Oklahoma State

Most fans at Oklahoma State games come from either Greater Tulsa or Greater Oklahoma City. Both cities are about an hour away from Stillwater, home of the Cowboys. So Oklahoma State tries to make it worth the trip and provide a game day, rather than just a game for their fans. There are live bands, food vendors, children's activities, disc jockeys, and live radio remote parking lot broadcasts for each home game. Tents are available for groups to rent for their tailgating. Some fraternities use them as well as businesses for corporate customers. The "Posse's Tent" is set up right next to the stadium offering a one dollar meal to all members. The meal consists of a grilled hot dog, chips and a soda.

Many fans, however, just show up in the parking lot and do their own thing. There are Cowboy Orange flags and happy tailgaters everywhere. Vans arrive early and the smell of barbecue hangs in the air. Since Oklahoma is the birthplace of barbecue sauce, Cowboy fans want to make sure it endures.

Face painting for children and good food and company make tailgating at Oklahoma State a family affair

About the Author

J oe Drozda has been an avid tailgater for better than a quarter of a century and has attended more than 50 college football games across the United States in the last four years alone. In preparation for this book, he interviewed hundreds of tailgaters, conducted surveys, took pictures and talked with almost all the major college athletic departments to become "the authority" on tailgating in America. He not only willingly traveled the country from Boston College to Southern Cal, but he also gave up his spot in the garage to store and test hundreds of gadgets for the betterment of tailgating.

"The Droz" has a B.S. in marketing from Indiana University and has written articles on unrelated topics ranging from management to college fund-raising.

Photography Credits:

Photos by Joe Drozda with the exception of the following:Page 13, all photos provided by Wilshire Fragrances, Inc.; page 15, provided by Georgia Sports Information; page 24, all photos provided by Turtle Top Vans; page 25, provided by Indiana Bureau of Motor Vehicles; page 38, provided by CANDEA Inc.; page 39, provided by Coleman; page 41 and 42, provided by Rubbermaid; page 43: photo in upper left provided by Coleman, art for Kingsford Charcoal provided by Kingsford, photo in lower right provided by Char-Broil; page 61, photo in far right provided by Coleman; page 74, all photos provided by Johnsonville Foods; page 77, cover art appears courtesy of *Financial World* magazine; page 78, courtesy of *Purdue Alumnus* magazine; page 96, provided by The Pasta Shoppe; page 97, provided by The Truxel's; page 104, cover art provided by Chapters Books; page 110, provided by The South Bend Chocolate Company; page 113, courtesy of *Purdue Alumnus* magazine; page 124-125, all logo art appears with the permission of the company; page 128-129, provided by Georgia Sports Information; page 131, photo by V. Scott Gilmore; page 132-133, provided by Illinois Sports Information; page 134, provided by Penn State Sports Information; page 135, provided by Michigan Sports Information; page 138, provided by Nebraska Sports Information; page 139, provided by Louisiana State Sports Information; page 140-141, provided by Clemson Sports Information ; page 142, provided by Indiana Sports Information; page 143, provided by Purdue Sports Information; page 144-145, provided by Cathy Robinson; page 146, provided by Florida Sports Information; page 147, provided by Auburn Sports Information; page 148, providedby Colorado Sports Information; page 149, provided by Maryland Sports Information; page 150-151, provided by Oregon Sports Inforation; page 152, photo by Steve Serio and provided by Northwestern Sports Information; page 154, provided by Iowa State Sports Information; page 155, provided by Mississippi Sports Information; page 156, provided by Wyoming Sports Information; page 157, provided by West Point's Sports Information; page 158, provided by East Carolina Sports Information; page 159, provided by North Carolina State Sports Information; page 160, provided by Air Force Academy Sports Information; page 161, provided by Texas Tech Sports Information; page 162, provided by Washington Sports Information; page 163, provided by Rice Sports Information; page 164, provided by Wake Forest Sports Information; page 165, provided by Georgia Tech Sports Information; page 166, provided by Iowa Sports Information; page 167, provided by Wisconsin Sports Information, page 168, provided by Michigan State Sports Information; page 169, provided by Tennessee Sports Information; page 170, provided by Northern Illinois Sports Information.